MAY 2013

Test Results for Digital Data Acquisition Tool:
FTK Imager CLI 2.9.0_Debian

NCJ 242138

Greg Ridgeway
Acting Director, National Institute of Justice

This report was prepared for the National Institute of Justice, U.S. Department of Justice, by the Office of Law Enforcement Standards of the National Institute of Standards and Technology under Interagency Agreement 2003–IJ–R–029.

The National Institute of Justice is a component of the Office of Justice Programs, which also includes the Bureau of Justice Assistance, the Bureau of Justice Statistics, the Office of Juvenile Justice and Delinquency Prevention, the Office for Victims of Crime, and the Office of Sex Offender Sentencing, Monitoring, Apprehending, Registering, and Tracking.

May 2013

Test Results for Digital Data Acquisition Tool:
FTK Imager CLI 2.9.0_Debian

**National Institute of
Standards and Technology**
U.S. Department of Commerce

Contents

Introduction

The Computer Forensics Tool Testing (CFTT) program is a joint project of the National Institute of Justice (NIJ), the Department of Homeland Security (DHS), and the National Institute of Standards and Technology Law Enforcement Standards Office (OLES) and Information Technology Laboratory (ITL). CFTT is supported by other organizations, including the Federal Bureau of Investigation, the U.S. Department of Defense Cyber Crime Center, U.S. Internal Revenue Service Criminal Investigation Division Electronic Crimes Program, and the U.S. Department of Homeland Security's Bureau of Immigration and Customs Enforcement, U.S. Customs and Border Protection and U.S. Secret Service. The objective of the CFTT program is to provide measurable assurance to practitioners, researchers and other applicable users that the tools used in computer forensics investigations provide accurate results. Accomplishing this requires the development of specifications and test methods for computer forensics tools and subsequent testing of specific tools against those specifications.

Test results provide the information necessary for developers to improve tools, users to make informed choices, and the legal community and others to understand the tools' capabilities. The CFTT approach to testing computer forensics tools is based on well-recognized methodologies for conformance and quality testing. The specifications and test methods are posted on the CFTT Web site (http://www.cftt.nist.gov/) for review and comment by the computer forensics community.

This document reports the results from testing FTK Imager CLI 2.9.0_Debian against the *Digital Data Acquisition Tool Assertions and Test Plan Version 1.0*, available at the CFTT Web site (http://www.cftt.nist.gov/DA-ATP-pc-01.pdf).

Test results from other tools can be found on NIJ's computer forensics tool testing Web page, http://www.ojp.usdoj.gov/nij/topics/technology/electronic-crime/cftt.htm.

How to Read This Report

This report is divided into five sections. The first section is a summary of the results from the test runs. This section is sufficient for most readers to assess the suitability of the tool for the intended use. The remaining sections of the report describe how the tests were conducted, discuss any anomalies that were encountered and provide documentation of test case run details that support the report summary. Section 2 gives justification for the selection of test cases from the set of possible cases defined in the test plan for Digital Data Acquisition tools. The test cases are selected, in general, based on features offered by the tool. Section 3 describes in more depth any anomalies summarized in the first section. Section 4 lists hardware and software used to run the test cases with links to additional information about the items used. Section 5 contains a description of each test case run. The description of each test run lists all test assertions used in the test case, the expected result and the actual result. Please refer to the vendor documentation for guidance on using the tool.

Test Results for Digital Data Acquisition Tool

Tool Tested:	FTK Imager CLI
Software Version:	2.9.0 Debian
Runtime Environment(s)	Debian Live 6.0.4 and Ubuntu 10.04 LTS
Supplier:	AccessData
Address:	384 South 400 West, Suite 200 Lindon, UT 84042 USA
Tel:	1-801-377-5410
Fax:	1-801-765-4370
E-mail:	support@accessdata.com
WWW:	http://accessdata.com/

1 Results Summary

AccessData's FTK Imager CLI v2.9 Debian is designed to image and restore hard drives and other secondary storage. It uses the Debian command line interface to image, clone and restore acquired data. Except for the case where a drive with faulty sectors was imaged (test case DA-09), the tool acquired all sectors of the test media completely and accurately. In test cases DA-04 and DA-17 that measure how a tool behaves when the destination media has insufficient space for a clone or restore task, the tool failed to display a message indicating that the destination drive had insufficient space.

Refer to sections 3.1 and 3.2 for additional details on test cases DA-04, DA-17 and DA-09.

2 Test Case Selection

Test cases used to test disk imaging tools are defined in *Digital Data Acquisition Tool Assertions and Test Plan Version 1.0*. To test a tool, test cases are selected from the *Test Plan* document based on the features offered by the tool. Not all test cases or test assertions are appropriate for all tools. There is a core set of base cases (e.g., DA-06 and DA-07) that are executed for every tool tested. Tool features guide the selection of additional test cases. If a given tool implements a feature, then the test cases linked to that feature are run. Table 1 lists the testable features of FTK Imager CLI v2.9 Debian and the linked test cases selected for execution. Table 2 lists the features not available in FTK Imager CLI v2.9 Debian and the test cases not executed.

Table 1. Selected Test Cases

Supported Optional Feature	Cases Selected for Execution
Create a clone during acquisition	01
Create an unaligned clone from a digital source	02

Supported Optional Feature	Cases Selected for Execution
Create a truncated clone from a physical device	04
Base Cases	06 & 07
Read error during acquisition	09
Create an image file in more than one format	10
Insufficient space for image file	12
Create a clone from an image file	14 & 17
Detect a corrupted (or changed) image file	24 & 25
Convert an image file from one format to another	26

Table 2. Omitted Test Cases

Unsupported Optional Feature	Cases Omitted (Not Executed)
Create cylinder aligned clones	03, 15, 21 & 23
Device I/O error generator available	05, 11 & 18
Create an image of a drive with hidden sectors	08
Destination Device Switching	13
Create a clone from a subset of an image file	16
Fill excess sectors on a clone acquisition	19
Fill excess sectors on a clone device	20, 21, 22 & 23

Some test cases have different forms to accommodate parameters within test assertions. These variations cover the acquisition interface to the source media, the type of digital object acquired and image file format.

The following source interfaces were tested: USB, ATA28, ATA48, FW, SATA28, SATA48 and SCSI. These are noted as variations on test cases DA-01 and DA-06.

The following digital source types were tested: partitions (FAT16, FAT32, NTFS, EXT3, EXT4), compact flash (CF) and thumb drive (Thumb). These digital source types are noted as variations on test cases DA-02 and DA–07.

The following image file types are supported by the tool: SMART ew-compressed, E01 and encrypted. These were tested as alternate image file formats and are noted as variations on test case DA-10.

3   Results by Test Assertion

A test assertion is a verifiable statement about a single condition after an action is performed by the tool under test. A test case usually checks a group of assertions after the action of a single execution of the tool under test. Test assertions are defined and linked to test cases in *Digital Data Acquisition Tool Assertions and Test Plan Version 1.0*. Table 3 summarizes the test results for all the test cases by assertion. The column labeled **Assertions Tested** gives the text of each assertion. The column labeled **Tests** gives the number of test cases that use the given assertion. The column labeled **Anomaly** gives the section number in this report where any observed anomalies are discussed.

Table 3. Assertions Tested

Assertions Tested	Tests	Anomaly
AM-01 The tool uses access interface SRC-AI to access the digital source.	33	
AM-02 The tool acquires digital source DS.	33	
AM-03 The tool executes in execution environment XE.	62	
AM-04 If clone creation is specified, the tool creates a clone of the digital source.	14	
AM-05 If image file creation is specified, the tool creates an image file on file system type FS.	19	
AM-06 All visible sectors are acquired from the digital source.	32	3.2
AM-08 All sectors acquired from the digital source are acquired accurately.	32	
AM-09 If unresolved errors occur while reading from the selected digital source, the tool notifies the user of the error type and location within the digital source.	1	3.2
AM-10 If unresolved errors occur while reading from the selected digital source, the tool uses a benign fill in the destination object in place of the inaccessible data.	1	
AO-01 If the tool creates an image file, the data represented by the image file is the same as the data acquired by the tool.	18	
AO-02 If an image file format is specified, the tool creates an image file in the specified format.	3	
AO-04 If the tool is creating an image file and there is insufficient space on the image destination device to contain the image file, the tool shall notify the user.	1	
AO-05 If the tool creates a multi-file image of a requested size then all the individual files shall be no larger than the requested size.	18	
AO-06 If the tool performs an image file integrity check on an image file that has not been changed since the file was created, the tool shall notify the user that the image file has not been changed.	1	
AO-07 If the tool performs an image file integrity check on an image file that has been changed since the file was created, the tool shall notify the user that the image file has been changed.	1	
AO-08 If the tool performs an image file integrity check on an image file that has been changed since the file was created, the tool shall notify the user of the affected locations.	1	
AO-09 If the tool converts a source image file from one format to a target image file in another format, the acquired data represented in the target image file is the same as the acquired data in the source image file.	9	
AO-11 If requested, a clone is created during an acquisition of a	14	

Assertions Tested	Tests	Anomaly
digital source.		
AO-12 If requested, a clone is created from an image file.	18	
AO-13 A clone is created using access interface DST-AI to write to the clone device.	32	
AO-14 If an unaligned clone is created, each sector written to the clone is accurately written to the same disk address on the clone that the sector occupied on the digital source.	31	
AO-17 If requested, any excess sectors on a clone destination device are not modified.	16	
AO-19 If there is insufficient space to create a complete clone, a truncated clone is created using all available sectors of the clone device.	2	
AO-20 If a truncated clone is created, the tool notifies the user.	2	3.1
AO-23 If the tool logs any log significant information, the information is accurately recorded in the log file.	62	
AO-24 If the tool executes in a forensically safe execution environment, the digital source is unchanged by the acquisition process.	33	

Two test assertions only apply in special circumstances. The assertion AO-22 is checked only for tools that create block hashes. The assertion AO-24 is only checked if the tool is executed in a run time environment that does not modify attached storage devices, such as MS-DOS. In normal operation, an imaging tool is used in conjunction with a write block device to protect the source drive. Table 4 lists the assertions that were not tested, usually due to the tool not supporting some optional feature, e.g., creation of cylinder-aligned clones.

Table 4. Assertions Not Tested

Assertions Not Tested
AM-07 All hidden sectors are acquired from the digital source.
AO-03 If there is an error while writing the image file, the tool notifies the user.
AO-10 If there is insufficient space to contain all files of a multi-file image and if destination device switching is supported, the image is continued on another device.
AO-15 If an aligned clone is created, each sector within a contiguous span of sectors from the source is accurately written to the same disk address on the clone device relative to the start of the span as the sector occupied on the original digital source. A span of sectors is defined to be either a mountable partition or a contiguous sequence of sectors not part of a mountable partition. Extended partitions, which may contain both mountable partitions and unallocated sectors, are not mountable partitions.
AO-16 If a subset of an image or acquisition is specified, all the subset is cloned.

Assertions Not Tested
AO-18 If requested, a benign fill is written to excess sectors of a clone.
AO-21 If there is a write error during clone creation, the tool notifies the user.
AO-22 If requested, the tool calculates block hashes for a specified block size during an acquisition for each block acquired from the digital source.

3.1 Creating truncated clones

Test case DA-04 measured FTK Imager CLI v2.9 Debian's behavior when asked to acquire a physical device to a truncated clone. Test case DA-17 tested the behavior for creating truncated clones from image files. In both cases the tool did not inform the user that a truncated clone had been created. The tests ended without any message informing the user that the destination drive was smaller than the source. The tool does not log progress information, to the screen or to file, during a clone operation. It appears that the message logging function of the tool is limited by scope to image acquisitions only.

3.2 Faulty sectors

When cloning a drive with faulty sectors, test case DA-09, the tool stopped the acquisition at the first faulty sector. No notification was given to the user.

4 Testing Environment

The tests were run in the NIST CFTT lab. This section describes the selected test execution environments, computers available for testing, using the support software, and notes on other test hardware.

4.1 Execution Environment

The tool was executed in the Debian Live 6.0.4 and Ubuntu 10.04 LTS environments.

4.2 Test Computers

Two computers were used to run the tool: **DeathStar and Frank**.

DeathStar has the following configuration:

TCP Custom Built
Processor, Intel Core i5-2500 3.3GHZ
Super Writemaster CDRW/DVD
BIOS Version ASUS EFI Version 9.16.2011

Frank has the following configuration:

Latitude D800
Processor, Intel Pentium 4 3.40GHZ
Assembly, Floppy Drive, 1.44M, 3.5"

Samsung CDRW/DVD
BIOS Version Inter Version BF865105

4.3 Support Software

A package of programs to support test analysis, FS-TST Release 2.0, was used. The software can be obtained from: http://www.cftt.nist.gov/diskimaging/fs-tst20.zip.

4.4 Test Drive Creation

There are three ways that a hard drive may be used in a tool test case: as a source drive that is imaged by the tool, as a media drive that contains image files created by the tool under test, or as a destination drive on which the tool under test creates a clone of the source drive. In addition to the operating system drive formatting tools, some tools (**diskwipe** and **diskhash**) from the FS-TST package are used to setup test drives.

4.4.1 Source Drive

The setup of most source drives follows the same general procedure, but there are several steps that may be varied depending on the needs of the test case.

1. The drive is filled with known data by the **diskwipe** program from FS-TST. The **diskwipe** program writes the sector address to each sector in both C/H/S and LBA format. The remainder of the sector bytes is set to a constant fill value unique for each drive. The fill value is noted in the **diskwipe** tool log file.
2. The drive may be formatted with partitions as required for the test case.
3. An operating system may optionally be installed.
4. A set of reference hashes is created by the FS-TST **diskhash** tool. These include both SHA1 and MD5 hashes. In addition to full drive hashes, hashes of each partition may also be computed.
5. If the drive is intended for hidden area tests (DA-08), an HPA, a DCO or both may be created. The **diskhash** tool is then used to calculate reference hashes of just the visible sectors of the drive.

The source drives for DA-09 are created such that there is a consistent set of faulty sectors on the drive. Each of these source drives is initialized with **diskwipe** and then their faulty sectors are activated. For each of these source drives, a duplicate drive with no faulty sectors serves as a reference drive for comparison.

4.4.2 Media Drive

To setup a media drive, the drive is formatted with one of the supported file systems. A media drive may be used in several test cases.

4.4.3 Destination Drive

To setup a destination drive, the drive is filled with known data by the **diskwipe** program from FS-TST. Partitions may be created if the test case involves restoring from the image of a logical acquire.

4.5 Test Drive Analysis

For test cases that create a clone of a physical device, e.g., DA-01, DA-04, etc., the destination drive is compared to the source drive with the **diskcmp** program from the FS-TST package; for test cases that create a clone of a logical device, i.e., a partition, e.g., DA-02, DA-20, etc., the destination partition is compared to the source partition with the **partcmp** program. For a destination created from an image file, e.g., DA-14, the destination is compared, using either **diskcmp** (for physical device clones) or **partcmp** (for partition clones), to the source that was acquired to create the image file. Both **diskcmp** and **partcmp** note differences between the source and destination. If the destination is larger than the source, it is scanned and the excess destination sectors are categorized as either undisturbed (still containing the fill pattern written by **diskwipe**), zero filled or changed to something else.

For test case DA-09, imaging a drive with known faulty sectors, the program **ana-bad** is used to compare the faulty sector reference drive to a cloned version of the faulty sector drive.

For test cases such as DA-06 and DA-07, any acquisition hash computed by the tool under test is compared to the reference hash of the source to check that the source is completely and accurately acquired.

4.6 Note on Test Drives

The testing uses several test drives from a variety of vendors. The drives are identified by an external label that consists of a two-digit hexadecimal value and an optional tag, e.g., 25-SATA. The combination of hex value and tag serves as a unique identifier for each drive. The two digit hex value is used by the FS-TST **diskwipe** program as a sector fill value. The FS-TST compare tools, **diskcmp** and **partcmp,** count sectors that are filled with the source and destination fill values on a destination that is larger than the original source.

5 Test Results

The main item of interest for interpreting the test results is determining the conformance of the tool under test with the test assertions. Conformance with each assertion tested by a given test case is evaluated by examining the **Log Highlights** box of the test report.

5.1 Test Results Report Key

The following table presents an explanation of each section of the test details in section 5.2. The Tester Name, Test Host, Test Date, Drives, Source Setup and Log Highlights sections for each test case are populated by excerpts taken from the log files produced by the tool under test and the FS-TST tools that were executed in support of test case setup and analysis.

Heading	Description
First Line:	Test case ID, name and version of tool tested.
Case Summary:	Test case summary from *Digital Data Acquisition Tool*

Heading	Description
	Assertions and Test Plan Version 1.0.
Assertions:	The test assertions applicable to the test case, selected from *Digital Data Acquisition Tool Assertions and Test Plan Version 1.0.*
Tester Name:	Name or initials of person executing test procedure.
Test Host:	Host computer executing the test.
Test Date:	Time and date that test was started.
Drives:	Source drive (the drive acquired), destination drive (if a clone is created) and media drive (to contain a created image).
Source Setup:	Layout of partitions on the source drive and the expected hash of the drive.
Log Highlights:	Information extracted from various log files to illustrate conformance or nonconformance to the test assertions.
Results	Expected and actual results for each assertion tested.
Analysis	Whether or not the expected results were achieved.

5.2 Test Details

The test results are presented in this section.

5.2.1 DA-01-ATA28

Test Case DA-01-ATA28 AccessData FTK Imager CLI v2.9	
Case Summary:	DA-01 Acquire a physical device using access interface AI to an unaligned clone.
Assertions:	AM-01 The tool uses access interface SRC-AI to access the digital source. AM-02 The tool acquires digital source DS. AM-03 The tool executes in execution environment XE. AM-04 If clone creation is specified, the tool creates a clone of the digital source. AM-06 All visible sectors are acquired from the digital source. AM-08 All sectors acquired from the digital source are acquired accurately. AO-11 If requested, a clone is created during an acquisition of a digital source. AO-13 A clone is created using access interface DST-AI to write to the clone device. AO-14 If an unaligned clone is created, each sector written to the clone is accurately written to the same disk address on the clone that the sector occupied on the digital source. AO-17 If requested, any excess sectors on a clone destination device are not modified. AO-22 If requested, the tool calculates block hashes for a specified block size during an acquisition for each block acquired from the digital source. AO-23 If the tool logs any log significant information, the information is accurately recorded in the log file. AO-24 If the tool executes in a forensically safe execution environment, the digital source is unchanged by the acquisition process.
Tester Name:	csr
Test Host:	DeathStar
Test Date:	Thu Aug 23 09:08:32 2012
Drives:	src(41) dst (24-LAP) other (none)
Source Setup:	src hash (SHA256): < FBF3AA21489653D880FFAE71449A9F7E8EE4F56A6C3BF58A3A3FFB13203F1B1D > src hash (SHA1): < 15CAA1A307271160D8372668BF8A03FC45A51CC9 > src hash (MD5): < 0A6A8EF78BDC14E2026710D8CCB5607C > 78125000 total sectors (40000000000 bytes) 65534/015/63 (max cyl/hd values) 65535/016/63 (number of cyl/hd) IDE disk: Model (WDC WD400BB-75JHC0) serial # (WD-WMAMC4658355) N Start LBA Length Start C/H/S End C/H/S boot Partition type 1 P 000000063 078107967 0000/001/01 1023/254/63 Boot 07 NTFS 2 P 000000000 000000000 0000/000/00 0000/000/00 00 empty entry 3 P 000000000 000000000 0000/000/00 0000/000/00 00 empty entry 4 P 000000000 000000000 0000/000/00 0000/000/00 00 empty entry 1 078107967 sectors 39991279104 bytes
Log Highlights:	====== Destination drive setup ====== 78140160 sectors wiped with 41 ====== Comparison of original to clone drive ====== Sectors compared: 78125000 Sectors match: 78125000 Sectors differ: 0 Bytes differ: 0 Diffs range Source (78125000) has 15160 fewer sectors than destination (78140160) Zero fill: 0 Src Byte fill (41): 15160 Dst Byte fill (24): 0 Other fill: 0 Other no fill: 0 Zero fill range: Src fill range: 78125000-78140159 Dst fill range: Other fill range: Other not filled range: 0 source read errors, 0 destination read errors

Test Case DA-01-ATA28 AccessData FTK Imager CLI v2.9	
	Write Block: 4 FASTBloc IDE OS: Linux debian 2.6.32-5-486 #1 Mon Oct 3 03:34:28 UTC 2011 i686 GNU/Linux
Results:	

Assertion & Expected Result	Actual Result
AM-01 Source acquired using interface AI.	as expected
AM-02 Source is type DS.	as expected
AM-03 Execution environment is XE.	as expected
AM-04 A clone is created.	as expected
AM-06 All visible sectors acquired.	as expected
AM-08 All sectors accurately acquired.	as expected
AO-11 A clone is created during acquisition.	as expected
AO-13 Clone created using interface AI.	as expected
AO-14 An unaligned clone is created.	as expected
AO-17 Excess sectors are unchanged.	as expected
AO-22 Tool calculates hashes by block.	option not available
AO-23 Logged information is correct.	as expected
AO-24 Source is unchanged by acquisition.	not checked

Analysis:	Expected results achieved

5.2.2 DA-01-ATA48

Test Case DA-01-ATA48 AccessData FTK Imager CLI v2.9	
Case Summary:	DA-01 Acquire a physical device using access interface AI to an unaligned clone.
Assertions:	AM-01 The tool uses access interface SRC-AI to access the digital source. AM-02 The tool acquires digital source DS. AM-03 The tool executes in execution environment XE. AM-04 If clone creation is specified, the tool creates a clone of the digital source. AM-06 All visible sectors are acquired from the digital source. AM-08 All sectors acquired from the digital source are acquired accurately. AO-11 If requested, a clone is created during an acquisition of a digital source. AO-13 A clone is created using access interface DST-AI to write to the clone device. AO-14 If an unaligned clone is created, each sector written to the clone is accurately written to the same disk address on the clone that the sector occupied on the digital source. AO-17 If requested, any excess sectors on a clone destination device are not modified. AO-22 If requested, the tool calculates block hashes for a specified block size during an acquisition for each block acquired from the digital source. AO-23 If the tool logs any log significant information, the information is accurately recorded in the log file. AO-24 If the tool executes in a forensically safe execution environment, the digital source is unchanged by the acquisition process.
Tester Name:	csr
Test Host:	DeathStar
Test Date:	Mon Jan 23 14:52:29 2012
Drives:	src(4E) dst (32-IDE) other (none)
Source Setup:	src hash (SHA1): < 7DDFF1A74B2E2B7E7EE43C41CD9066E27986644D > src hash (MD5): < 62C9436930204E0F38921771ACA1BB88 > 488397168 total sectors (250059350016 bytes) 30400/254/63 (max cyl/hd values) 30401/255/63 (number of cyl/hd) IDE disk: Model (WDC WD2500JB-22FUA0) serial # (WD-WMAEP1925256) N Start LBA Length Start C/H/S End C/H/S boot Partition type 1 P 000000063 488375937 0000/001/01 1023/254/63 Boot 07 NTFS 2 P 000000000 000000000 0000/000/00 0000/000/00 00 empty entry 3 P 000000000 000000000 0000/000/00 0000/000/00 00 empty entry 4 P 000000000 000000000 0000/000/00 0000/000/00 00 empty entry 1 488375937 sectors 250048479744 bytes
Log Highlights:	====== Destination drive setup ====== 488397168 sectors wiped with 32 ====== Comparison of original to clone drive ====== Sectors compared: 488397168 Sectors match: 488397168 Sectors differ: 0 Bytes differ: 0 Diffs range 0 source read errors, 0 destination read errors Write Block: 4 FASTBloc IDE OS: Linux ubuntu 2.6.32-33-generic #70-Ubuntu SMP Thu Jul 7 21:09:46 UTC 2011 i686 GNU/Linux
Results:	

Assertion & Expected Result	Actual Result
AM-01 Source acquired using interface AI.	as expected
AM-02 Source is type DS.	as expected
AM-03 Execution environment is XE.	as expected
AM-04 A clone is created.	as expected
AM-06 All visible sectors acquired.	as expected

Test Case DA-01-ATA48 AccessData FTK Imager CLI v2.9		
	AM-08 All sectors accurately acquired.	as expected
	AO-11 A clone is created during acquisition.	as expected
	AO-13 Clone created using interface AI.	as expected
	AO-14 An unaligned clone is created.	as expected
	AO-17 Excess sectors are unchanged.	as expected
	AO-22 Tool calculates hashes by block.	option not available
	AO-23 Logged information is correct.	as expected
	AO-24 Source is unchanged by acquisition.	not checked
Analysis:	Expected results achieved	

5.2.3 DA-01-FW

Test Case DA-01-FW AccessData FTK Imager CLI v2.9	
Case Summary:	DA-01 Acquire a physical device using access interface AI to an unaligned clone.
Assertions:	AM-01 The tool uses access interface SRC-AI to access the digital source. AM-02 The tool acquires digital source DS. AM-03 The tool executes in execution environment XE. AM-04 If clone creation is specified, the tool creates a clone of the digital source. AM-06 All visible sectors are acquired from the digital source. AM-08 All sectors acquired from the digital source are acquired accurately. AO-11 If requested, a clone is created during an acquisition of a digital source. AO-13 A clone is created using access interface DST-AI to write to the clone device. AO-14 If an unaligned clone is created, each sector written to the clone is accurately written to the same disk address on the clone that the sector occupied on the digital source. AO-17 If requested, any excess sectors on a clone destination device are not modified. AO-22 If requested, the tool calculates block hashes for a specified block size during an acquisition for each block acquired from the digital source. AO-23 If the tool logs any log significant information, the information is accurately recorded in the log file. AO-24 If the tool executes in a forensically safe execution environment, the digital source is unchanged by the acquisition process.
Tester Name:	csr
Test Host:	DeathStar
Test Date:	Wed Feb 1 10:01:22 2012
Drives:	src(63-FU2) dst (30-IDE) other (none)
Source Setup:	src hash (SHA256): < EC8EF011494BA6DA18F74C47547C3E74E7180585096A830F9247A98EF613BB1D > src hash (SHA1): < F7069EDCBEAC863C88DECED82159F22DA96BE99B > src hash (MD5): < EE217BC4FA4F3D1B4021D29B065AA9EC > 117304992 total sectors (60060155904 bytes) Model (SP0612N) serial # () N Start LBA Length Start C/H/S End C/H/S boot Partition type 1 P 000000063 004192902 0000/001/01 0260/254/63 Boot 06 Fat16 2 X 004192965 113097600 0261/000/01 1023/254/63 0F extended 3 S 000000063 113097537 0261/001/01 1023/254/63 0B Fat32 4 S 000000000 000000000 0000/000/00 0000/000/00 00 empty entry 5 P 000000000 000000000 0000/000/00 0000/000/00 00 empty entry 6 P 000000000 000000000 0000/000/00 0000/000/00 00 empty entry 1 004192902 sectors 2146765824 bytes 3 113097537 sectors 57905938944 bytes
Log Highlights:	====== Destination drive setup ====== 156301488 sectors wiped with 30 ====== Comparison of original to clone drive ====== Sectors compared: 117304992 Sectors match: 117304992 Sectors differ: 0 Bytes differ: 0 Diffs range Source (117304992) has 38996496 fewer sectors than destination (156301488) Zero fill: 0 Src Byte fill (63): 0 Dst Byte fill (30): 38996496 Other fill: 0 Other no fill: 0 Zero fill range: Src fill range: Dst fill range: 117304992-156301487 Other fill range: Other not filled range:

Test Case DA-01-FW AccessData FTK Imager CLI v2.9		
	0 source read errors, 0 destination read errors ====== Tool Settings: ====== fill: none Write Block: 64 Tableau Forensic FireWire Brigde OS: Linux ubuntu 2.6.32-33-generic #70-Ubuntu SMP Thu Jul 7 21:09:46 UTC 2011 i686 GNU/Linux	
Results:		

Assertion & Expected Result	Actual Result
AM-01 Source acquired using interface AI.	as expected
AM-02 Source is type DS.	as expected
AM-03 Execution environment is XE.	as expected
AM-04 A clone is created.	as expected
AM-06 All visible sectors acquired.	as expected
AM-08 All sectors accurately acquired.	as expected
AO-11 A clone is created during acquisition.	as expected
AO-13 Clone created using interface AI.	as expected
AO-14 An unaligned clone is created.	as expected
AO-17 Excess sectors are unchanged.	as expected
AO-22 Tool calculates hashes by block.	option not available
AO-23 Logged information is correct.	as expected
AO-24 Source is unchanged by acquisition.	not checked

Analysis:	Expected results achieved

5.2.4 DA-01-SATA28

Test Case DA-01-SATA28 AccessData FTK Imager CLI v2.9	
Case Summary:	DA-01 Acquire a physical device using access interface AI to an unaligned clone.
Assertions:	AM-01 The tool uses access interface SRC-AI to access the digital source. AM-02 The tool acquires digital source DS. AM-03 The tool executes in execution environment XE. AM-04 If clone creation is specified, the tool creates a clone of the digital source. AM-06 All visible sectors are acquired from the digital source. AM-08 All sectors acquired from the digital source are acquired accurately. AO-11 If requested, a clone is created during an acquisition of a digital source. AO-13 A clone is created using access interface DST-AI to write to the clone device. AO-14 If an unaligned clone is created, each sector written to the clone is accurately written to the same disk address on the clone that the sector occupied on the digital source. AO-17 If requested, any excess sectors on a clone destination device are not modified. AO-22 If requested, the tool calculates block hashes for a specified block size during an acquisition for each block acquired from the digital source. AO-23 If the tool logs any log significant information, the information is accurately recorded in the log file. AO-24 If the tool executes in a forensically safe execution environment, the digital source is unchanged by the acquisition process.
Tester Name:	csr
Test Host:	DeathStar
Test Date:	Tue Jan 24 12:33:55 2012
Drives:	src(07-SATA) dst (32-SATA) other (none)

Source Setup:	src hash (SHA256): < CE65C4A3C3164D3EBAD58D33BB2415D29E260E1F88DC5A131B1C4C9C2945B8A9 >
	src hash (SHA1): < 655E9BDDB36A3F9C5C4CC8BF32B8C5B41AF9F52E >
	src hash (MD5): < 2EAF712DAD80F66E30DEA00365B4579B >
	156301488 total sectors (80026361856 bytes)
	Model (WDC WD800JD-32HK) serial # (WD-WMAJ91510044)
	  N Start LBA Length Start C/H/S End C/H/S boot Partition type
	  1 P 000000063 156280257 0000/001/01 1023/254/63 Boot 07 NTFS
	  2 P 000000000 000000000 0000/000/00 0000/000/00 00 empty entry
	  3 P 000000000 000000000 0000/000/00 0000/000/00 00 empty entry
	  4 P 000000000 000000000 0000/000/00 0000/000/00 00 empty entry
	1 156280257 sectors 80015491584 bytes

Log Highlights:	====== Destination drive setup ====== 156301488 sectors wiped with 32 ====== Comparison of original to clone drive ====== Sectors compared: 156301488 Sectors match: 156301488 Sectors differ: 0 Bytes differ: 0 Diffs range 0 source read errors, 0 destination read errors Write Block: none OS: Linux ubuntu 2.6.32-33-generic #70-Ubuntu SMP Thu Jul 7 21:09:46 UTC 2011 i686 GNU/Linux ====== Source drive rehash ====== Rehash (SHA1) of source: 655E9BDDB36A3F9C5C4CC8BF32B8C5B41AF9F52E
Results:	

Assertion & Expected Result	Actual Result
AM-01 Source acquired using interface AI.	as expected

	AM-02 Source is type DS.	as expected
	AM-03 Execution environment is XE.	as expected
	AM-04 A clone is created.	as expected
	AM-06 All visible sectors acquired.	as expected
	AM-08 All sectors accurately acquired.	as expected
	AO-11 A clone is created during acquisition.	as expected
	AO-13 Clone created using interface AI.	as expected
	AO-14 An unaligned clone is created.	as expected
	AO-17 Excess sectors are unchanged.	as expected
	AO-22 Tool calculates hashes by block.	option not available
	AO-23 Logged information is correct.	as expected
	AO-24 Source is unchanged by acquisition.	as expected
Analysis:	Expected results achieved	

5.2.5 DA-01-SATA48

Test Case DA-01-SATA48 AccessData FTK Imager CLI v2.9

Case Summary:	DA-01 Acquire a physical device using access interface AI to an unaligned clone.
Assertions:	AM-01 The tool uses access interface SRC-AI to access the digital source. AM-02 The tool acquires digital source DS. AM-03 The tool executes in execution environment XE. AM-04 If clone creation is specified, the tool creates a clone of the digital source. AM-06 All visible sectors are acquired from the digital source. AM-08 All sectors acquired from the digital source are acquired accurately. AO-11 If requested, a clone is created during an acquisition of a digital source. AO-13 A clone is created using access interface DST-AI to write to the clone device. AO-14 If an unaligned clone is created, each sector written to the clone is accurately written to the same disk address on the clone that the sector occupied on the digital source. AO-17 If requested, any excess sectors on a clone destination device are not modified. AO-22 If requested, the tool calculates block hashes for a specified block size during an acquisition for each block acquired from the digital source. AO-23 If the tool logs any log significant information, the information is accurately recorded in the log file. AO-24 If the tool executes in a forensically safe execution environment, the digital source is unchanged by the acquisition process.
Tester Name:	csr
Test Host:	DeathStar
Test Date:	Tue Jan 24 16:15:39 2012
Drives:	src(0D-SATA) dst (5B-IDE) other (none)
Source Setup:	src hash (SHA1): < BAAD80E8781E55F2E3EF528CA73BD41D228C1377 > src hash (MD5): < 1FA7C3CBE60EB9E89863DED2411E40C9 > 488397168 total sectors (250059350016 bytes) 30400/254/63 (max cyl/hd values) 30401/255/63 (number of cyl/hd) Model (WDC WD2500JD-22F) serial # (WD-WMAEH2678216) N Start LBA Length Start C/H/S End C/H/S boot Partition type 1 P 000000063 488375937 0000/001/01 1023/254/63 Boot 07 NTFS 2 P 000000000 000000000 0000/000/00 0000/000/00 00 empty entry 3 P 000000000 000000000 0000/000/00 0000/000/00 00 empty entry 4 P 000000000 000000000 0000/000/00 0000/000/00 00 empty entry 1 488375937 sectors 250048479744 bytes
Log Highlights:	====== Destination drive setup ====== 488397168 sectors wiped with 5B ====== Comparison of original to clone drive ====== Sectors compared: 488397168 Sectors match: 488397168 Sectors differ: 0 Bytes differ: 0 Diffs range 0 source read errors, 0 destination read errors Write Block: none OS: Linux ubuntu 2.6.32-33-generic #70-Ubuntu SMP Thu Jul 7 21:09:46 UTC 2011 i686 GNU/Linux ====== Source drive rehash ====== Rehash (SHA1) of source: BAAD80E8781E55F2E3EF528CA73BD41D228C1377

Results:	Assertion & Expected Result	Actual Result
	AM-01 Source acquired using interface AI.	as expected
	AM-02 Source is type DS.	as expected

Test Case DA-01-SATA48 AccessData FTK Imager CLI v2.9		
	AM-03 Execution environment is XE.	as expected
	AM-04 A clone is created.	as expected
	AM-06 All visible sectors acquired.	as expected
	AM-08 All sectors accurately acquired.	as expected
	AO-11 A clone is created during acquisition.	as expected
	AO-13 Clone created using interface AI.	as expected
	AO-14 An unaligned clone is created.	as expected
	AO-17 Excess sectors are unchanged.	as expected
	AO-22 Tool calculates hashes by block.	option not available
	AO-23 Logged information is correct.	as expected
	AO-24 Source is unchanged by acquisition.	as expected
Analysis:	Expected results achieved	

5.2.6 DA-01-SCSI

Test Case DA-01-SCSI AccessData FTK Imager CLI v2.9	
Case Summary:	DA-01 Acquire a physical device using access interface AI to an unaligned clone.
Assertions:	AM-01 The tool uses access interface SRC-AI to access the digital source. AM-02 The tool acquires digital source DS. AM-03 The tool executes in execution environment XE. AM-04 If clone creation is specified, the tool creates a clone of the digital source. AM-06 All visible sectors are acquired from the digital source. AM-08 All sectors acquired from the digital source are acquired accurately. AO-11 If requested, a clone is created during an acquisition of a digital source. AO-13 A clone is created using access interface DST-AI to write to the clone device. AO-14 If an unaligned clone is created, each sector written to the clone is accurately written to the same disk address on the clone that the sector occupied on the digital source. AO-17 If requested, any excess sectors on a clone destination device are not modified. AO-22 If requested, the tool calculates block hashes for a specified block size during an acquisition for each block acquired from the digital source. AO-23 If the tool logs any log significant information, the information is accurately recorded in the log file. AO-24 If the tool executes in a forensically safe execution environment, the digital source is unchanged by the acquisition process.
Tester Name:	csr
Test Host:	DeathStar
Test Date:	Wed Jan 25 15:47:14 2012
Drives:	src(2A) dst (8A) other (none)
Source Setup:	src hash (SHA256): < AE8E839101661367D92803D5F5D408268635EFD8A05FEA633838CDC3919F5ABA > src hash (SHA1): < F5F9F2903DCAB895F36E270FB22A722E27918125 > src hash (MD5): < 91E0AC905F682ECF6DE4E9835089B519 > 17783249 total sectors (9105023488 bytes) Model (QM39100TD-SCA) serial # (PCB=20-116711-06 HDAQM39100TD-SCA) N Start LBA Length Start C/H/S End C/H/S boot Partition type 1 P 000000063 017751762 0000/001/01 1023/254/63 Boot 07 NTFS 2 P 000000000 000000000 0000/000/00 0000/000/00 00 empty entry 3 P 000000000 000000000 0000/000/00 0000/000/00 00 empty entry 4 P 000000000 000000000 0000/000/00 0000/000/00 00 empty entry 1 017751762 sectors 9088902144 bytes
Log Highlights:	====== Destination drive setup ====== 39102336 sectors wiped with 8A ====== Comparison of original to clone drive ====== Sectors compared: 17783249 Sectors match: 17783249 Sectors differ: 0 Bytes differ: 0 Diffs range Source (17783249) has 21319087 fewer sectors than destination (39102336) Zero fill: 0 Src Byte fill (2A): 0 Dst Byte fill (8A): 21319087 Other fill: 0 Other no fill: 0 Zero fill range: Src fill range: Dst fill range: 17783249-39102335 Other fill range: Other not filled range: 0 source read errors, 0 destination read errors Write Block: none

Test Case DA-01-SCSI AccessData FTK Imager CLI v2.9	
	OS: Linux ubuntu 2.6.32-33-generic #70-Ubuntu SMP Thu Jul 7 21:09:46 UTC 2011 i686 GNU/Linux ====== Source drive rehash ====== Rehash (SHA1) of source: F5F9F2903DCAB895F36E270FB22A722E27918125
Results:	

Assertion & Expected Result	Actual Result
AM-01 Source acquired using interface AI.	as expected
AM-02 Source is type DS.	as expected
AM-03 Execution environment is XE.	as expected
AM-04 A clone is created.	as expected
AM-06 All visible sectors acquired.	as expected
AM-08 All sectors accurately acquired.	as expected
AO-11 A clone is created during acquisition.	as expected
AO-13 Clone created using interface AI.	as expected
AO-14 An unaligned clone is created.	as expected
AO-17 Excess sectors are unchanged.	as expected
AO-22 Tool calculates hashes by block.	option not available
AO-23 Logged information is correct.	as expected
AO-24 Source is unchanged by acquisition.	as expected

Analysis:	Expected results achieved

5.2.7 DA-01-USB

Test Case DA-01-USB AccessData FTK Imager CLI v2.9	
Case Summary:	DA-01 Acquire a physical device using access interface AI to an unaligned clone.
Assertions:	AM-01 The tool uses access interface SRC-AI to access the digital source. AM-02 The tool acquires digital source DS. AM-03 The tool executes in execution environment XE. AM-04 If clone creation is specified, the tool creates a clone of the digital source. AM-06 All visible sectors are acquired from the digital source. AM-08 All sectors acquired from the digital source are acquired accurately. AO-11 If requested, a clone is created during an acquisition of a digital source. AO-13 A clone is created using access interface DST-AI to write to the clone device. AO-14 If an unaligned clone is created, each sector written to the clone is accurately written to the same disk address on the clone that the sector occupied on the digital source. AO-17 If requested, any excess sectors on a clone destination device are not modified. AO-22 If requested, the tool calculates block hashes for a specified block size during an acquisition for each block acquired from the digital source. AO-23 If the tool logs any log significant information, the information is accurately recorded in the log file. AO-24 If the tool executes in a forensically safe execution environment, the digital source is unchanged by the acquisition process.
Tester Name:	csr
Test Host:	DeathStar
Test Date:	Thu Feb 2 07:30:49 2012
Drives:	src(63-FU2) dst (84-FU2) other (none)

Source Setup:	src hash (SHA256): <
	EC8EF011494BA6DA18F74C47547C3E74E7180585096A830F9247A98EF613BB1D >
	src hash (SHA1): < F7069EDCBEAC863C88DECED82159F22DA96BE99B >
	src hash (MD5): < EE217BC4FA4F3D1B4021D29B065AA9EC >
	117304992 total sectors (60060155904 bytes)
	Model (SP0612N) serial # ()
	<pre>N Start LBA Length Start C/H/S End C/H/S boot Partition type
	1 P 000000063 004192902 0000/001/01 0260/254/63 Boot 06 Fat16
	2 X 004192965 113097600 0261/000/01 1023/254/63 0F extended
	3 S 000000063 113097537 0261/001/01 1023/254/63 0B Fat32
	4 S 000000000 000000000 0000/000/00 0000/000/00 00 empty entry
	5 P 000000000 000000000 0000/000/00 0000/000/00 00 empty entry
	6 P 000000000 000000000 0000/000/00 0000/000/00 00 empty entry
	1 004192902 sectors 2146765824 bytes
	3 113097537 sectors 57905938944 bytes</pre>

Log Highlights:	====== Destination drive setup ====== 160836480 sectors wiped with 84 ====== Comparison of original to clone drive ====== Sectors compared: 117304992 Sectors match: 117304992 Sectors differ: 0 Bytes differ: 0 Diffs range Source (117304992) has 43531488 fewer sectors than destination (160836480) Zero fill: 0 Src Byte fill (63): 0 Dst Byte fill (84): 43531488 Other fill: 0 Other no fill: 0 Zero fill range: Src fill range: Dst fill range: 117304992-160836479 Other fill range: Other not filled range:

0 source read errors, 0 destination read errors

====== Tool Settings: ======
fill: none

Write Block: 18 Tableau Forensic USB Brigde/Ultrablock USB

OS: Linux debian 2.6.32-5-486 #1 Mon Oct 3 03:34:28 UTC 2011 i686 GNU/Linux

Results:

Assertion & Expected Result	Actual Result
AM-01 Source acquired using interface AI.	as expected
AM-02 Source is type DS.	as expected
AM-03 Execution environment is XE.	as expected
AM-04 A clone is created.	as expected
AM-06 All visible sectors acquired.	as expected
AM-08 All sectors accurately acquired.	as expected
AO-11 A clone is created during acquisition.	as expected
AO-13 Clone created using interface AI.	as expected
AO-14 An unaligned clone is created.	as expected
AO-17 Excess sectors are unchanged.	as expected
AO-22 Tool calculates hashes by block.	option not available
AO-23 Logged information is correct.	as expected
AO-24 Source is unchanged by acquisition.	not checked

Analysis: Expected results achieved

5.2.8 DA-02-CF

Test Case DA-02-CF AccessData FTK Imager CLI v2.9	
Case Summary:	DA-02 Acquire a digital source of type DS to an unaligned clone.
Assertions:	AM-01 The tool uses access interface SRC-AI to access the digital source. AM-02 The tool acquires digital source DS. AM-03 The tool executes in execution environment XE. AM-04 If clone creation is specified, the tool creates a clone of the digital source. AM-06 All visible sectors are acquired from the digital source. AM-08 All sectors acquired from the digital source are acquired accurately. AO-11 If requested, a clone is created during an acquisition of a digital source. AO-13 A clone is created using access interface DST-AI to write to the clone device. AO-14 If an unaligned clone is created, each sector written to the clone is accurately written to the same disk address on the clone that the sector occupied on the digital source. AO-17 If requested, any excess sectors on a clone destination device are not modified. AO-22 If requested, the tool calculates block hashes for a specified block size during an acquisition for each block acquired from the digital source. AO-23 If the tool logs any log significant information, the information is accurately recorded in the log file. AO-24 If the tool executes in a forensically safe execution environment, the digital source is unchanged by the acquisition process.
Tester Name:	csr
Test Host:	DeathStar
Test Date:	Tue Feb 14 08:41:00 2012
Drives:	src(C1-CF) dst (C2-CF) other (none)
Source Setup:	src hash (SHA256): < C7CF0218222DF80D5316511D6814266C7FA507C13F795AD3D323BB73C1590D80 > src hash (SHA1): < 5B8235178DF99FA307430C088F81746606638A0B > src hash (MD5): < 776DF8B4D2589E21DEBCF589EDC16D78 > 503808 total sectors (257949696 bytes) Model (CF) serial # () N Start LBA Length Start C/H/S End C/H/S boot Partition type 1 P 778135908 1141509631 0357/116/40 0357/032/45 Boot 72 other 2 P 168689522 1936028240 0288/115/43 0367/114/50 Boot 65 other 3 P 1869881465 1936028192 0366/032/33 0357/032/43 Boot 79 other 4 P 2885681152 000055499 0372/097/50 0000/010/00 Boot 0D other 1 1141509631 sectors 584452931072 bytes 2 1936028240 sectors 991246458880 bytes 3 1936028192 sectors 991246434304 bytes 4 000055499 sectors 28415488 bytes
Log Highlights:	====== Destination drive setup ====== 503808 sectors wiped with C2 ====== Comparison of original to clone drive ====== Sectors compared: 503808 Sectors match: 503808 Sectors differ: 0 Bytes differ: 0 Diffs range 0 source read errors, 0 destination read errors Write Block: 7 UltraBlock Forensic Card Reader OS: Linux debian 2.6.32-5-486 #1 Mon Oct 3 03:34:28 UTC 2011 i686 GNU/Linux
Results:	

Assertion & Expected Result	Actual Result
AM-01 Source acquired using interface AI.	as expected
AM-02 Source is type DS.	as expected

Test Case DA-02-CF AccessData FTK Imager CLI v2.9		
	AM-03 Execution environment is XE.	as expected
	AM-04 A clone is created.	as expected
	AM-06 All visible sectors acquired.	as expected
	AM-08 All sectors accurately acquired.	as expected
	AO-11 A clone is created during acquisition.	as expected
	AO-13 Clone created using interface AI.	as expected
	AO-14 An unaligned clone is created.	as expected
	AO-17 Excess sectors are unchanged.	as expected
	AO-22 Tool calculates hashes by block.	option not available
	AO-23 Logged information is correct.	as expected
	AO-24 Source is unchanged by acquisition.	not checked
Analysis:	Expected results achieved	

5.2.9 DA-02-EXT3

Test Case DA-02-EXT3 AccessData FTK Imager CLI v2.9	
Case Summary:	DA-02 Acquire a digital source of type DS to an unaligned clone.
Assertions:	AM-01 The tool uses access interface SRC-AI to access the digital source. AM-02 The tool acquires digital source DS. AM-03 The tool executes in execution environment XE. AM-04 If clone creation is specified, the tool creates a clone of the digital source. AM-06 All visible sectors are acquired from the digital source. AM-08 All sectors acquired from the digital source are acquired accurately. AO-11 If requested, a clone is created during an acquisition of a digital source. AO-13 A clone is created using access interface DST-AI to write to the clone device. AO-14 If an unaligned clone is created, each sector written to the clone is accurately written to the same disk address on the clone that the sector occupied on the digital source. AO-17 If requested, any excess sectors on a clone destination device are not modified. AO-22 If requested, the tool calculates block hashes for a specified block size during an acquisition for each block acquired from the digital source. AO-23 If the tool logs any log significant information, the information is accurately recorded in the log file. AO-24 If the tool executes in a forensically safe execution environment, the digital source is unchanged by the acquisition process.
Tester Name:	csr
Test Host:	DeathStar
Test Date:	Wed Apr 11 08:33:43 2012
Drives:	src(49-SATA) dst (6F) other (none)
Source Setup:	src hash (SHA1): < 6EC98F42EB5914D1F9D1661C0BB0A3660569F95B > src hash (MD5): < 30BAB74F67783C0555BCBD73DD4D0D5E > 156301488 total sectors (80026361856 bytes) Model (ST380815AS) serial # (5QZ5TD8Y) N Start LBA Length Start C/H/S End C/H/S boot Partition type 1 P 000002048 010485760 0000/032/33 0652/213/09 07 NTFS 2 P 010490445 005863725 0653/000/01 1017/254/63 83 Linux 3 P 016354170 007807590 1018/000/01 1023/254/63 83 Linux 4 P 000000000 000000000 0000/000/00 0000/000/00 00 empty entry 1 010485760 sectors 5368709120 bytes 2 005863725 sectors 3002227200 bytes 3 007807590 sectors 3997486080 bytes 49-SATAEXT3-md5sum 5863725 A25176AE775F65181DAC8C8D051DDF5D 49-SATAEXT3-sha1sum 5863725 FDF0F2BA2D4CB2D45E45717213AE218880236418 Excess destination partition sectors hash: SHA1 3002227200 - 3224277503 = 7D266425BAC55D10000F60978253ACFFABC24F97
Log Highlights:	====== Destination drive setup ====== 120103200 sectors wiped with 6F ====== Comparison of original to clone drive ====== Sectors compared: 5863725 Sectors match: 5863725 Sectors differ: 0 Bytes differ: 0 Diffs range: Source (5863725) has 433692 fewer sectors than destination (6297417) Zero fill: 8081 Src Byte fill (49): 0 Dst Byte fill (6F): 425588 Other fill: 19 Other no fill: 4 Zero fill range: 6029313-6029320, 6029328-6033263, 6291464, 6291472-6295407, 6297216-6297415 Src fill range: Dst fill range: 5863725-6029311, 6033264-6291455, 6295408-6297215, 6297416 Other fill range: 6029322-6029327, 6291457-6291463,

```
6291466-6291471
Other not filled range:  6029312, 6029321, 6291456,
6291465
run start Mon Apr 16 08:44:14 2012
run finish Mon Apr 16 08:46:38 2012
elapsed time 0:2:24
Normal exit


====== Tool Settings: ======
fill: none

Write Block: 11 UltraBlock-SATA

OS: Linux debian 2.6.32-5-486 #1 Mon Oct 3 03:34:28 UTC 2011 i686 GNU/Linux


Excess destination partition sectors hash:
SHA1 3002227200 - 3224277503 = 7D266425BAC55D10000F60978253ACFFABC24F97

====== Source drive rehash ======
Rehash (SHA1) of source: 6EC98F42EB5914D1F9D1661C0BB0A3660569F95B
```

Results:

Assertion & Expected Result	Actual Result
AM-01 Source acquired using interface AI.	as expected
AM-02 Source is type DS.	as expected
AM-03 Execution environment is XE.	as expected
AM-04 A clone is created.	as expected
AM-06 All visible sectors acquired.	as expected
AM-08 All sectors accurately acquired.	as expected
AO-11 A clone is created during acquisition.	as expected
AO-13 Clone created using interface AI.	as expected
AO-14 An unaligned clone is created.	as expected
AO-17 Excess sectors are unchanged.	as expected
AO-22 Tool calculates hashes by block.	option not available
AO-23 Logged information is correct.	as expected
AO-24 Source is unchanged by acquisition.	as expected

Analysis: Expected results achieved

5.2.10   DA-02-EXT4

Test Case DA-02-EXT4 AccessData FTK Imager CLI v2.9	
Case Summary:	DA-02 Acquire a digital source of type DS to an unaligned clone.
Assertions:	AM-01 The tool uses access interface SRC-AI to access the digital source. AM-02 The tool acquires digital source DS. AM-03 The tool executes in execution environment XE. AM-04 If clone creation is specified, the tool creates a clone of the digital source. AM-06 All visible sectors are acquired from the digital source. AM-08 All sectors acquired from the digital source are acquired accurately. AO-11 If requested, a clone is created during an acquisition of a digital source. AO-13 A clone is created using access interface DST-AI to write to the clone device. AO-14 If an unaligned clone is created, each sector written to the clone is accurately written to the same disk address on the clone that the sector occupied on the digital source. AO-17 If requested, any excess sectors on a clone destination device are not modified. AO-22 If requested, the tool calculates block hashes for a specified block size during an acquisition for each block acquired from the digital source. AO-23 If the tool logs any log significant information, the information is accurately recorded in the log file. AO-24 If the tool executes in a forensically safe execution environment, the digital source is unchanged by the acquisition process.
Tester Name:	csr
Test Host:	DeathStar
Test Date:	Wed Apr 16 12:07:43 2012
Drives:	src(49-SATA) dst (6F) other (none)
Source Setup:	src hash (SHA1): < 6EC98F42EB5914D1F9D1661C0BB0A3660569F95B > src hash (MD5): < 30BAB74F67783C0555BCBD73DD4D0D5E > 156301488 total sectors (80026361856 bytes) Model (ST380815AS) serial # (5QZ5TD8Y) N Start LBA Length Start C/H/S End C/H/S boot Partition type 1 P 000002048 010485760 0000/032/33 0652/213/09 07 NTFS 2 P 010490445 005863725 0653/000/01 1017/254/63 83 Linux 3 P 016354170 007807590 1018/000/01 1023/254/63 83 Linux 4 P 000000000 000000000 0000/000/00 0000/000/00 00 empty entry 1 010485760 sectors 5368709120 bytes 2 005863725 sectors 3002227200 bytes 3 007807590 sectors 3997486080 bytes 49-SATAEXT4-md5sum 7807590 567F2826AB468D69F97CB0D1878BE25D 49-SATAEXT4-sha1sum 7807590 F28A79F5E5CD28F859A1AC6B18A2CA3682D15A2A Excess destination partition sectors hash: SHA1 3997486080 - 4293563903 = 6C3ED4F22307CC6A655A26688BA5732C0F88AB0C
Log Highlights:	====== Destination drive setup ====== 120103200 sectors wiped with 6F ====== Comparison of original to clone drive ====== Sectors compared: 7807590 Sectors match: 7807590 Sectors differ: 0 Bytes differ: 0 Diffs range: Source (7807590) has 578277 fewer sectors than destination (8385867) Zero fill: 200 Src Byte fill (49): 0 Dst Byte fill (6F): 578077 Other fill: 0 Other no fill: 0 Zero fill range: 8385664-8385863 Src fill range: Dst fill range: 7807590-8385663, 8385864-8385866 Other fill range: Other not filled range: run start Mon Apr 16 12:32:39 2012

```
run finish Mon Apr 16 12:35:28 2012
elapsed time 0:2:49
Normal exit


====== Tool Settings: ======
fill: none

Write Block: 11 UltraBlock-SATA

OS: Linux debian 2.6.32-5-486 #1 Mon Oct 3 03:34:28 UTC 2011 i686 GNU/Linux


Excess destination partition sectors hash:
SHA1 3997486080 - 4293563903 = 6C3ED4F22307CC6A655A26688BA5732C0F88AB0C

====== Source drive rehash ======
Rehash (SHA1) of source: 6EC98F42EB5914D1F9D1661C0BB0A3660569F95B
```

Results:

Assertion & Expected Result	Actual Result
AM-01 Source acquired using interface AI.	as expected
AM-02 Source is type DS.	as expected
AM-03 Execution environment is XE.	as expected
AM-04 A clone is created.	as expected
AM-06 All visible sectors acquired.	as expected
AM-08 All sectors accurately acquired.	as expected
AO-11 A clone is created during acquisition.	as expected
AO-13 Clone created using interface AI.	as expected
AO-14 An unaligned clone is created.	as expected
AO-17 Excess sectors are unchanged.	as expected
AO-22 Tool calculates hashes by block.	option not available
AO-23 Logged information is correct.	as expected
AO-24 Source is unchanged by acquisition.	as expected

Analysis: Expected results achieved

5.2.11   DA-02-F32

Test Case DA-02-F32 AccessData FTK Imager CLI v2.9	
Case Summary:	DA-02 Acquire a digital source of type DS to an unaligned clone.
Assertions:	AM-01 The tool uses access interface SRC-AI to access the digital source. AM-02 The tool acquires digital source DS. AM-03 The tool executes in execution environment XE. AM-04 If clone creation is specified, the tool creates a clone of the digital source. AM-06 All visible sectors are acquired from the digital source. AM-08 All sectors acquired from the digital source are acquired accurately. AO-11 If requested, a clone is created during an acquisition of a digital source. AO-13 A clone is created using access interface DST-AI to write to the clone device. AO-14 If an unaligned clone is created, each sector written to the clone is accurately written to the same disk address on the clone that the sector occupied on the digital source. AO-17 If requested, any excess sectors on a clone destination device are not modified. AO-22 If requested, the tool calculates block hashes for a specified block size during an acquisition for each block acquired from the digital source. AO-23 If the tool logs any log significant information, the information is accurately recorded in the log file. AO-24 If the tool executes in a forensically safe execution environment, the digital source is unchanged by the acquisition process.
Tester Name:	csr
Test Host:	DeathStar
Test Date:	Fri Feb 3 10:30:34 2012
Drives:	src(01-IDE) dst (4D-SATA) other (none)
Source Setup:	src hash (SHA1): < A48BB5665D6DC57C22DB68E2F723DA9AA8DF82B9 > src hash (MD5): < F458F673894753FA6A0EC8B8EC63848E > 78165360 total sectors (40020664320 bytes) Model (0BB-00JHC0) serial # (WD-WMAMC74171) N Start LBA Length Start C/H/S End C/H/S boot Partition type 1 P 000000063 020980827 0000/001/01 1023/254/63 0C Fat32X 2 X 020980890 057175335 1023/000/01 1023/254/63 0F extended 3 S 000000063 000032067 1023/001/01 1023/254/63 01 Fat12 4 x 000032130 002104515 1023/000/01 1023/254/63 05 extended 5 S 000000063 002104452 1023/001/01 1023/254/63 06 Fat16 6 x 002136645 004192965 1023/000/01 1023/254/63 05 extended 7 S 000000063 004192902 1023/001/01 1023/254/63 16 other 8 x 006329610 008401995 1023/000/01 1023/254/63 05 extended 9 S 000000063 008401932 1023/001/01 1023/254/63 0B Fat32 10 x 014731605 010490445 1023/000/01 1023/254/63 05 extended 11 S 000000063 010490382 1023/001/01 1023/254/63 83 Linux 12 x 025222050 004209030 1023/000/01 1023/254/63 05 extended 13 S 000000063 004208967 1023/001/01 1023/254/63 82 Linux swap 14 x 029431080 027744255 1023/000/01 1023/254/63 05 extended 15 S 000000063 027744192 1023/001/01 1023/254/63 07 NTFS 16 S 000000000 000000000 0000/000/00 0000/000/00 00 empty entry 17 P 000000000 000000000 0000/000/00 0000/000/00 00 empty entry 18 P 000000000 000000000 0000/000/00 0000/000/00 00 empty entry 1 020980827 sectors 10742183424 bytes 3 000032067 sectors 16418304 bytes 5 002104452 sectors 1077479424 bytes 7 004192902 sectors 2146765824 bytes 9 008401932 sectors 4301789184 bytes 11 010490382 sectors 5371075584 bytes 13 004208967 sectors 2154991104 bytes 15 027744192 sectors 14205026304 bytes 01F32-md5 4301789183 BFF7DC64C54339DA2A9D7972C076B514 01F32-sha1 4301789183 B861D9E999F39750B484FFB693FF69DEC090C6B8 01F32-sha256 4301789183 CAE3A4CC33D59548063255D2AA4016940AC712DD96985AD9B94FF271CC3E943E

Test Case DA-02-F32 AccessData FTK Imager CLI v2.9

Log Highlights:	====== Destination drive setup ====== 156301488 sectors wiped with 4D ====== Comparison of original to clone drive ====== Sectors compared: 8401932 Sectors match: 8401932 Sectors differ: 0 Bytes differ: 0 Diffs range: run start Tue Feb 14 07:43:54 2012 run finish Tue Feb 14 07:46:00 2012 elapsed time 0:2:6 Normal exit Write Block: 3 FASTbloc IDE OS: Linux debian 2.6.32-5-486 #1 Mon Oct 3 03:34:28 UTC 2011 i686 GNU/Linux

Results:		
	Assertion & Expected Result	**Actual Result**
	AM-01 Source acquired using interface AI.	as expected
	AM-02 Source is type DS.	as expected
	AM-03 Execution environment is XE.	as expected
	AM-04 A clone is created.	as expected
	AM-06 All visible sectors acquired.	as expected
	AM-08 All sectors accurately acquired.	as expected
	AO-11 A clone is created during acquisition.	as expected
	AO-13 Clone created using interface AI.	as expected
	AO-14 An unaligned clone is created.	as expected
	AO-17 Excess sectors are unchanged.	as expected
	AO-22 Tool calculates hashes by block.	option not available
	AO-23 Logged information is correct.	as expected
	AO-24 Source is unchanged by acquisition.	not checked

Analysis:	Expected results achieved

5.2.12   DA-02-NT

Test Case DA-02-NT AccessData FTK Imager CLI v2.9	
Case Summary:	DA-02 Acquire a digital source of type DS to an unaligned clone.
Assertions:	AM-01 The tool uses access interface SRC-AI to access the digital source. AM-02 The tool acquires digital source DS. AM-03 The tool executes in execution environment XE. AM-04 If clone creation is specified, the tool creates a clone of the digital source. AM-06 All visible sectors are acquired from the digital source. AM-08 All sectors acquired from the digital source are acquired accurately. AO-11 If requested, a clone is created during an acquisition of a digital source. AO-13 A clone is created using access interface DST-AI to write to the clone device. AO-14 If an unaligned clone is created, each sector written to the clone is accurately written to the same disk address on the clone that the sector occupied on the digital source. AO-17 If requested, any excess sectors on a clone destination device are not modified. AO-22 If requested, the tool calculates block hashes for a specified block size during an acquisition for each block acquired from the digital source. AO-23 If the tool logs any log significant information, the information is accurately recorded in the log file. AO-24 If the tool executes in a forensically safe execution environment, the digital source is unchanged by the acquisition process.
Tester Name:	csr
Test Host:	DeathStar
Test Date:	Thu Mar 1 13:10:10 2012
Drives:	src(01-IDE) dst (4D-SATA) other (none)

Source Setup:	src hash (SHA1): < A48BB5665D6DC57C22DB68E2F723DA9AA8DF82B9 >
	src hash (MD5): < F458F673894753FA6A0EC8B8EC63848E >
	78165360 total sectors (40020664320 bytes)
	Model (0BB-00JHC0) serial # (WD-WMAMC74171)
	  N Start LBA Length Start C/H/S End C/H/S boot Partition type
	  1 P 000000063 020980827 0000/001/01 1023/254/63 0C Fat32X
	  2 X 020980890 057175335 1023/000/01 1023/254/63 0F extended
	  3 S 000000063 000032067 1023/001/01 1023/254/63 01 Fat12
	  4 x 000032130 002104515 1023/000/01 1023/254/63 05 extended
	  5 S 000000063 002104452 1023/001/01 1023/254/63 06 Fat16
	  6 x 002136645 004192965 1023/000/01 1023/254/63 05 extended
	  7 S 000000063 004192902 1023/001/01 1023/254/63 16 other
	  8 x 006329610 008401995 1023/000/01 1023/254/63 05 extended
	  9 S 000000063 008401932 1023/001/01 1023/254/63 0B Fat32
	10 x 014731605 010490445 1023/000/01 1023/254/63 05 extended
	11 S 000000063 010490382 1023/001/01 1023/254/63 83 Linux
	12 x 025222050 004209030 1023/000/01 1023/254/63 05 extended
	13 S 000000063 004208967 1023/001/01 1023/254/63 82 Linux swap
	14 x 029431080 027744255 1023/000/01 1023/254/63 05 extended
	15 S 000000063 027744192 1023/001/01 1023/254/63 07 NTFS
	16 S 000000000 000000000 0000/000/00 0000/000/00 00 empty entry
	17 P 000000000 000000000 0000/000/00 0000/000/00 00 empty entry
	18 P 000000000 000000000 0000/000/00 0000/000/00 00 empty entry
	 1 020980827 sectors 10742183424 bytes
	 3 000032067 sectors 16418304 bytes
	 5 002104452 sectors 1077479424 bytes
	 7 004192902 sectors 2146765824 bytes
	 9 008401932 sectors 4301789184 bytes
	11 010490382 sectors 5371075584 bytes
	13 004208967 sectors 2154991104 bytes
	15 027744192 sectors 14205026304 bytes
	01NT-md5 14205026303 92B27B30BEE8B0FFBA8C660FA1590D49
	Excess destination partition sectors hash:
	SHA1 14205026304 - 28410052607 = DFB523B023E56C64400736E404B362DE3FD6B828

Log Highlights:	====== Destination drive setup ====== 156301488 sectors wiped with 4D

```
====== Comparison of original to clone drive ======
Sectors compared:     27744192
Sectors match:        27744192
Sectors differ:              0
Bytes differ:                0
Diffs range:
Source (27744192) has 78140160 fewer sectors than destination (105884352)
Zero fill:     3295
Src Byte fill (01): 0
Dst Byte fill (4D): 78136568
Other fill:     4
Other no fill: 293
Zero fill range:  52942181-52942245, 52942265-52942271,
52942273-52942458, 52942465-52943886, 52943888-52945502
Src fill range:
Dst fill range:  27744192-52942167, 52942247, 52945760-105884350
Other fill range:  52942460-52942463
Other not filled range:  52942168-52942180, 52942246,
52942248-52942264, 52942272, 52942459, 52942464, 52943887,
52945503-52945759, 105884351
run start Fri Mar  2 15:45:31 2012
run finish Fri Mar  2 16:04:02 2012
elapsed time 0:18:31
Normal exit


====== Tool Settings: ======
fill: none

Write Block: 3 FASTBloc IDE

OS: Linux ubuntu 2.6.32-33-generic #70-Ubuntu SMP Thu Jul 7 21:09:46 UTC
2011 i686 GNU/Linux


Excess destination partition sectors hash:
SHA1 14205026304 - 28410052607 = DFB523B023E56C64400736E404B362DE3FD6B828
```

Results:		
	Assertion & Expected Result	Actual Result
	AM-01 Source acquired using interface AI.	as expected
	AM-02 Source is type DS.	as expected
	AM-03 Execution environment is XE.	as expected
	AM-04 A clone is created.	as expected
	AM-06 All visible sectors acquired.	as expected
	AM-08 All sectors accurately acquired.	as expected
	AO-11 A clone is created during acquisition.	as expected
	AO-13 Clone created using interface AI.	as expected
	AO-14 An unaligned clone is created.	as expected
	AO-17 Excess sectors are unchanged.	as expected
	AO-22 Tool calculates hashes by block.	option not available
	AO-23 Logged information is correct.	as expected
	AO-24 Source is unchanged by acquisition.	not checked

Analysis:	Expected results achieved

5.2.13 DA-02-THUMB

Test Case DA-02-THUMB AccessData FTK Imager CLI v2.9	
Case Summary:	DA-02 Acquire a digital source of type DS to an unaligned clone.
Assertions:	AM-01 The tool uses access interface SRC-AI to access the digital source. AM-02 The tool acquires digital source DS. AM-03 The tool executes in execution environment XE. AM-04 If clone creation is specified, the tool creates a clone of the digital source. AM-06 All visible sectors are acquired from the digital source. AM-08 All sectors acquired from the digital source are acquired accurately. AO-11 If requested, a clone is created during an acquisition of a digital source. AO-13 A clone is created using access interface DST-AI to write to the clone device. AO-14 If an unaligned clone is created, each sector written to the clone is accurately written to the same disk address on the clone that the sector occupied on the digital source. AO-17 If requested, any excess sectors on a clone destination device are not modified. AO-22 If requested, the tool calculates block hashes for a specified block size during an acquisition for each block acquired from the digital source. AO-23 If the tool logs any log significant information, the information is accurately recorded in the log file. AO-24 If the tool executes in a forensically safe execution environment, the digital source is unchanged by the acquisition process.
Tester Name:	csr
Test Host:	DeathStar
Test Date:	Wed Feb 15 08:39:02 2012
Drives:	src(D5-THUMB) dst (D6-THUMB) other (none)
Source Setup:	src hash (SHA1): < D68520EF74A336E49DCCF83815B7B08FDC53E38A > src hash (MD5): < C843593624B2B3B878596D8760B19954 > 505856 total sectors (258998272 bytes) Model (usb2.0Flash Disk) serial # ()
Log Highlights:	====== Destination drive setup ====== 4001760 sectors wiped with D6 ====== Comparison of original to clone drive ====== Sectors compared: 505856 Sectors match: 505856 Sectors differ: 0 Bytes differ: 0 Diffs range Source (505856) has 3495904 fewer sectors than destination (4001760) Zero fill: 0 Src Byte fill (D5): 0 Dst Byte fill (D6): 3495904 Other fill: 0 Other no fill: 0 Zero fill range: Src fill range: Dst fill range: 505856-4001759 Other fill range: Other not filled range: 0 source read errors, 0 destination read errors Write Block: 18 UltraBlock USB
Results:	

Assertion & Expected Result	Actual Result
AM-01 Source acquired using interface AI.	as expected
AM-02 Source is type DS.	as expected
AM-03 Execution environment is XE.	as expected
AM-04 A clone is created.	as expected
AM-06 All visible sectors acquired.	as expected

Test Case DA-02-THUMB AccessData FTK Imager CLI v2.9		
	AM-08 All sectors accurately acquired.	as expected
	AO-11 A clone is created during acquisition.	as expected
	AO-13 Clone created using interface AI.	as expected
	AO-14 An unaligned clone is created.	as expected
	AO-17 Excess sectors are unchanged.	as expected
	AO-22 Tool calculates hashes by block.	option not available
	AO-23 Logged information is correct.	as expected
	AO-24 Source is unchanged by acquisition.	not checked
Analysis:	Expected results achieved	

5.2.14   DA-04

Test Case DA-04 AccessData FTK Imager CLI v2.9	
Case Summary:	DA-04 Acquire a physical device to a truncated clone.
Assertions:	AM-01 The tool uses access interface SRC-AI to access the digital source. AM-02 The tool acquires digital source DS. AM-03 The tool executes in execution environment XE. AM-04 If clone creation is specified, the tool creates a clone of the digital source. AM-06 All visible sectors are acquired from the digital source. AM-08 All sectors acquired from the digital source are acquired accurately. AO-11 If requested, a clone is created during an acquisition of a digital source. AO-13 A clone is created using access interface DST-AI to write to the clone device. AO-14 If an unaligned clone is created, each sector written to the clone is accurately written to the same disk address on the clone that the sector occupied on the digital source. AO-19 If there is insufficient space to create a complete clone, a truncated clone is created using all available sectors of the clone device. AO-20 If a truncated clone is created, the tool notifies the user. AO-22 If requested, the tool calculates block hashes for a specified block size during an acquisition for each block acquired from the digital source. AO-23 If the tool logs any log significant information, the information is accurately recorded in the log file. AO-24 If the tool executes in a forensically safe execution environment, the digital source is unchanged by the acquisition process.
Tester Name:	csr
Test Host:	DeathStar
Test Date:	Fri Jan 27 07:47:47 2012
Drives:	src(4f) dst (31-IDE) other (none)
Source Setup:	src hash (SHA1): < 51FE53FD6BF7B7B69A875EDBD9AC01D41194C78C > src hash (MD5): < A98DF276339451CE9E701D087E2BFC95 > 488397168 total sectors (250059350016 bytes) 30400/254/63 (max cyl/hd values) 30401/255/63 (number of cyl/hd) IDE disk: Model (WDC WD2500JB-00EVA0) serial # (WD-WMAEH2681554) N Start LBA Length Start C/H/S End C/H/S boot Partition type 1 P 000000063 268413957 0000/001/01 1023/254/63 Boot 07 NTFS 2 P 000000000 000000000 0000/000/00 0000/000/00 00 empty entry 3 P 000000000 000000000 0000/000/00 0000/000/00 00 empty entry 4 P 000000000 000000000 0000/000/00 0000/000/00 00 empty entry 1 268413957 sectors 137427945984 bytes
Log Highlights:	====== Destination drive setup ====== 35673120 sectors wiped with 31 ====== Comparison of original to clone drive ====== Sectors compared: 35673120 Sectors match: 35673120 Sectors differ: 0 Bytes differ: 0 Diffs range Source (488397168) has 452724048 more sectors than destination (35673120) 0 source read errors, 0 destination read errors ====== Tool Message: ====== no message Write Block: 3 Fastbloc IDE OS: Linux ubuntu 2.6.32-33-generic #70-Ubuntu SMP Thu Jul 7 21:09:46 UTC 2011 i686 GNU/Linux
Results:	
		Assertion & Expected Result	Actual Result	

Test Case DA-04 AccessData FTK Imager CLI v2.9		
	AM-01 Source acquired using interface AI.	as expected
	AM-02 Source is type DS.	as expected
	AM-03 Execution environment is XE.	as expected
	AM-04 A clone is created.	as expected
	AM-06 All visible sectors acquired.	as expected
	AM-08 All sectors accurately acquired.	as expected
	AO-11 A clone is created during acquisition.	as expected
	AO-13 Clone created using interface AI.	as expected
	AO-14 An unaligned clone is created.	as expected
	AO-19 Truncated clone is created.	as expected
	AO-20 User notified that clone is truncated.	No Message
	AO-22 Tool calculates hashes by block.	option not available
	AO-23 Logged information is correct.	as expected
	AO-24 Source is unchanged by acquisition.	not checked
Analysis:	Expected results not achieved	

5.2.15   DA-06-ATA28

Test Case DA-06-ATA28 AccessData FTK Imager CLI v2.9	
Case Summary:	DA-06 Acquire a physical device using access interface AI to an image file.
Assertions:	AM-01 The tool uses access interface SRC-AI to access the digital source. AM-02 The tool acquires digital source DS. AM-03 The tool executes in execution environment XE. AM-05 If image file creation is specified, the tool creates an image file on file system type FS. AM-06 All visible sectors are acquired from the digital source. AM-08 All sectors acquired from the digital source are acquired accurately. AO-01 If the tool creates an image file, the data represented by the image file is the same as the data acquired by the tool. AO-05 If the tool creates a multi-file image of a requested size then all the individual files shall be no larger than the requested size. AO-22 If requested, the tool calculates block hashes for a specified block size during an acquisition for each block acquired from the digital source. AO-23 If the tool logs any log significant information, the information is accurately recorded in the log file. AO-24 If the tool executes in a forensically safe execution environment, the digital source is unchanged by the acquisition process.
Tester Name:	csr
Test Host:	DeathStar
Test Date:	Thu Aug 23 11:54:13 2012
Drives:	src(41) dst (none) other (0F-FU)
Source Setup:	src hash (SHA256): < FBF3AA21489653D880FFAE71449A9F7E8EE4F56A6C3BF58A3A3FFB13203F1B1D > src hash (SHA1): < 15CAA1A307271160D8372668BF8A03FC45A51CC9 > src hash (MD5): < 0A6A8EF78BDC14E2026710D8CCB5607C > 78125000 total sectors (40000000000 bytes) 65534/015/63 (max cyl/hd values) 65535/016/63 (number of cyl/hd) IDE disk: Model (WDC WD400BB-75JHC0) serial # (WD-WMAMC4658355) N Start LBA Length Start C/H/S End C/H/S boot Partition type 1 P 000000063 078107967 0000/001/01 1023/254/63 Boot 07 NTFS 2 P 000000000 000000000 0000/000/00 0000/000/00 00 empty entry 3 P 000000000 000000000 0000/000/00 0000/000/00 00 empty entry 4 P 000000000 000000000 0000/000/00 0000/000/00 00 empty entry 1 078107967 sectors 39991279104 bytes

Log Highlights:	====== Tool Settings: ======
	image size: 952647655 MB
	image format: E01
	
	Write Block: 4 FASTBLOC IDE
	
	OS: Linux debian 2.6.32-5-486 #1 Mon Oct 3 03:34:28 UTC 2011 i686 GNU/Linux
	
	====== Image file segments ======
	    1 952647655 2012-08-23 12:18 da-06-ata28.E01
	    2 1112 2012-08-23 12:21 da-06-ata28.E01.txt
	======= Excerpt from Tool log ========
	Case: da-06-ata28
	Drive Geometry:
	 Cylinders: 4863
	 Heads: 255
	 Sectors per Track: 63
	 Bytes per Sector: 512
	 Sector Count: 78125000
	Physical Drive Information:
	 Drive Model: ATA WDC WD400BB-75JH
	 Drive Interface Type: SCSI
	 Source data size: 38146 MB
	 Sector count: 78125000

Test Case DA-06-ATA28 AccessData FTK Imager CLI v2.9	

	Source hash:
	  MD5: 0a6a8ef78bdc14e2026710d8ccb5607c
	  SHA1: 15caa1a307271160d8372668bf8a03fc45a51cc9
	Verification hash:
	  MD5: 0a6a8ef78bdc14e2026710d8ccb5607c
	  SHA1: 15caa1a307271160d8372668bf8a03fc45a51cc9
	Segment list:
	  /media/cftt/da-06-ata28.E01
	======== End of Excerpt from Tool log ========

Results:	

Assertion & Expected Result	Actual Result
AM-01 Source acquired using interface AI.	as expected
AM-02 Source is type DS.	as expected
AM-03 Execution environment is XE.	as expected
AM-05 An image is created on file system type FS.	as expected
AM-06 All visible sectors acquired.	as expected
AM-08 All sectors accurately acquired.	as expected
AO-01 Image file is complete and accurate.	as expected
AO-05 Multifile image created.	as expected
AO-22 Tool calculates hashes by block.	option not available
AO-23 Logged information is correct.	as expected
AO-24 Source is unchanged by acquisition.	not checked

Analysis:	Expected results achieved

5.2.16   DA-06-ATA48

Test Case DA-06-ATA48 AccessData FTK Imager CLI v2.9	
Case Summary:	DA-06 Acquire a physical device using access interface AI to an image file.
Assertions:	AM-01 The tool uses access interface SRC-AI to access the digital source. AM-02 The tool acquires digital source DS. AM-03 The tool executes in execution environment XE. AM-05 If image file creation is specified, the tool creates an image file on file system type FS. AM-06 All visible sectors are acquired from the digital source. AM-08 All sectors acquired from the digital source are acquired accurately. AO-01 If the tool creates an image file, the data represented by the image file is the same as the data acquired by the tool. AO-05 If the tool creates a multi-file image of a requested size then all the individual files shall be no larger than the requested size. AO-22 If requested, the tool calculates block hashes for a specified block size during an acquisition for each block acquired from the digital source. AO-23 If the tool logs any log significant information, the information is accurately recorded in the log file. AO-24 If the tool executes in a forensically safe execution environment, the digital source is unchanged by the acquisition process.
Tester Name:	csr
Test Host:	DeathStar
Test Date:	Wed Mar 7 07:32:15 2012
Drives:	src(4F) dst (none) other (5D-SATA)
Source Setup:	src hash (SHA1): < 51FE53FD6BF7B7B69A875EDBD9AC01D41194C78C > src hash (MD5): < A98DF276339451CE9E701D087E2BFC95 > 488397168 total sectors (250059350016 bytes) 30400/254/63 (max cyl/hd values) 30401/255/63 (number of cyl/hd) IDE disk: Model (WDC WD2500JB-00EVA0) serial # (WD-WMAEH2681554) N Start LBA Length Start C/H/S End C/H/S boot Partition type 1 P 000000063 268413957 0000/001/01 1023/254/63 Boot 07 NTFS 2 P 000000000 000000000 0000/000/00 0000/000/00 00 empty entry 3 P 000000000 000000000 0000/000/00 0000/000/00 00 empty entry 4 P 000000000 000000000 0000/000/00 0000/000/00 00 empty entry 1 268413957 sectors 137427945984 bytes

Log Highlights:	====== Destination drive setup ======
	625142448 sectors wiped with 5D
	Write Block: 3 FASTBloc IDE
	
	OS: Linux ubuntu 2.6.32-33-generic #70-Ubuntu SMP Thu Jul 7 21:09:46 UTC 2011 i686 GNU/Linux
	
	====== Image file segments ======
	    1 2147411976 2012-03-07 14:50 da-06-ata48.s01
	    2 1143 2012-03-07 15:59 da-06-ata48.s01.txt
	    3 2015779044 2012-03-07 15:42 da-06-ata48.s02
	    4 16384 2012-03-07 14:15 lost+found
	    5 0 2012-03-07 16:00 ls.txt
	======== Excerpt from Tool log ========
	Case: da-06-ata48
	Drive Geometry:
	 Cylinders: 30401
	 Heads: 255
	 Sectors per Track: 63
	 Bytes per Sector: 512
	 Sector Count: 488397168
	Physical Drive Information:
	 Drive Model: ATA WDC WD2500JB-00E
	 Drive Interface Type: SCSI
	 Source data size: 238475 MB
	 Sector count: 488397168
	Source hash:
	 MD5: a98df276339451ce9e701d087e2bfc95

Test Case DA-06-ATA48 AccessData FTK Imager CLI v2.9

```
         SHA1:    51fe53fd6bf7b7b69a875edbd9ac01d41194c78c
         Verification hash:
          MD5:    a98df276339451ce9e701d087e2bfc95
          SHA1:    51fe53fd6bf7b7b69a875edbd9ac01d41194c78c
         Segment list:
           /media/xxx/da-06-ata48.s01
           /media/xxx/da-06-ata48.s02
         ======== End of Excerpt from Tool log ========
```

Results:

Assertion & Expected Result	Actual Result
AM-01 Source acquired using interface AI.	as expected
AM-02 Source is type DS.	as expected
AM-03 Execution environment is XE.	as expected
AM-05 An image is created on file system type FS.	as expected
AM-06 All visible sectors acquired.	as expected
AM-08 All sectors accurately acquired.	as expected
AO-01 Image file is complete and accurate.	as expected
AO-05 Multifile image created.	as expected
AO-22 Tool calculates hashes by block.	option not available
AO-23 Logged information is correct.	as expected
AO-24 Source is unchanged by acquisition.	not checked

Analysis: Expected results achieved

5.2.17   DA-06-FW

Test Case DA-06-FW AccessData FTK Imager CLI v2.9	
Case Summary:	DA-06 Acquire a physical device using access interface AI to an image file.
Assertions:	AM-01 The tool uses access interface SRC-AI to access the digital source. AM-02 The tool acquires digital source DS. AM-03 The tool executes in execution environment XE. AM-05 If image file creation is specified, the tool creates an image file on file system type FS. AM-06 All visible sectors are acquired from the digital source. AM-08 All sectors acquired from the digital source are acquired accurately. AO-01 If the tool creates an image file, the data represented by the image file is the same as the data acquired by the tool. AO-05 If the tool creates a multi-file image of a requested size then all the individual files shall be no larger than the requested size. AO-22 If requested, the tool calculates block hashes for a specified block size during an acquisition for each block acquired from the digital source. AO-23 If the tool logs any log significant information, the information is accurately recorded in the log file. AO-24 If the tool executes in a forensically safe execution environment, the digital source is unchanged by the acquisition process.
Tester Name:	csr
Test Host:	DeathStar
Test Date:	Wed Mar 14 10:22:01 2012
Drives:	src(01-SATA) dst (none) other (5D-SATA)
Source Setup:	src hash (SHA256): < 1AA01FEAE55F5CD55185D2B1A1359B3F913E7093FEF1D1ADA220CAC456BA40D8 > src hash (SHA1): < 4951236428C36B944E62E8D65862DCBEF05F282C > src hash (MD5): < 0A49B13D91FA9DA87CEEE9D006CB6FD6 > 156301488 total sectors (80026361856 bytes) Model (0JD-32HKA0) serial # (WD-WMAJ91448529)

Log Highlights:	====== Destination drive setup ======
	625142448 sectors wiped with 5D
	
	====== Tool Settings: ======
	image size:4G
	image format: dd
	
	OS: Linux ubuntu 2.6.32-33-generic #70-Ubuntu SMP Thu Jul 7 21:09:46 UTC 2011 i686 GNU/Linux
	
	====== Image file segments ======
	    1 4294967296 2012-03-15 07:21 da-06-fw.001
	    2 1573 2012-03-15 08:34 da-06-fw.001.txt
	    3 4294967296 2012-03-15 07:25 da-06-fw.002
	  . . .
	   18 4294967296 2012-03-15 08:19 da-06-fw.018
	   19 2716950528 2012-03-15 08:21 da-06-fw.019
	   20 16384 2012-03-15 11:09 lost+found
	======== Excerpt from Tool log ========
	Case: da-06-fw
	Drive Geometry:
	 Cylinders: 9729
	 Heads: 255
	 Sectors per Track: 63
	 Bytes per Sector: 512
	 Sector Count: 156301488
	Physical Drive Information:
	 Drive Model: WDC WD80 0JD-32HKA0
	 Drive Interface Type: SCSI
	 Source data size: 76319 MB
	 Sector count: 156301488
	Source hash:
	 MD5: 0a49b13d91fa9da87ceee9d006cb6fd6

```
      SHA1:    4951236428c36b944e62e8d65862dcbef05f282c
Verification hash:
MD5:      0a49b13d91fa9da87ceee9d006cb6fd6
 SHA1:    4951236428c36b944e62e8d65862dcbef05f282c
Segment list:
  /media/xxx/da-06-fw.001
  /media/xxx/da-06-fw.002
  /media/xxx/da-06-fw.003
  /media/xxx/da-06-fw.004
  /media/xxx/da-06-fw.005
  /media/xxx/da-06-fw.006
  /media/xxx/da-06-fw.007
  /media/xxx/da-06-fw.008
  /media/xxx/da-06-fw.009
  /media/xxx/da-06-fw.010
  /media/xxx/da-06-fw.011
  /media/xxx/da-06-fw.012
  /media/xxx/da-06-fw.013
  /media/xxx/da-06-fw.014
  /media/xxx/da-06-fw.015
  /media/xxx/da-06-fw.016
  /media/xxx/da-06-fw.017
  /media/xxx/da-06-fw.018
  /media/xxx/da-06-fw.019
======== End of Excerpt from Tool log ========
```

Results:

Assertion & Expected Result	Actual Result
AM-01 Source acquired using interface AI.	as expected
AM-02 Source is type DS.	as expected
AM-03 Execution environment is XE.	as expected
AM-05 An image is created on file system type FS.	as expected
AM-06 All visible sectors acquired.	as expected
AM-08 All sectors accurately acquired.	as expected
AO-01 Image file is complete and accurate.	as expected
AO-05 Multifile image created.	as expected
AO-22 Tool calculates hashes by block.	option not available
AO-23 Logged information is correct.	as expected
AO-24 Source is unchanged by acquisition.	not checked

Analysis: Expected results achieved

5.2.18   DA-06-SATA28

Test Case DA-06-SATA28 AccessData FTK Imager CLI v2.9	
Case Summary:	DA-06 Acquire a physical device using access interface AI to an image file.
Assertions:	AM-01 The tool uses access interface SRC-AI to access the digital source. AM-02 The tool acquires digital source DS. AM-03 The tool executes in execution environment XE. AM-05 If image file creation is specified, the tool creates an image file on file system type FS. AM-06 All visible sectors are acquired from the digital source. AM-08 All sectors acquired from the digital source are acquired accurately. AO-01 If the tool creates an image file, the data represented by the image file is the same as the data acquired by the tool. AO-05 If the tool creates a multi-file image of a requested size then all the individual files shall be no larger than the requested size. AO-22 If requested, the tool calculates block hashes for a specified block size during an acquisition for each block acquired from the digital source. AO-23 If the tool logs any log significant information, the information is accurately recorded in the log file. AO-24 If the tool executes in a forensically safe execution environment, the digital source is unchanged by the acquisition process.
Tester Name:	csr
Test Host:	DeathStar
Test Date:	Wed Feb 22 12:48:36 2012
Drives:	src(4B-SATA) dst (none) other (5D-SATA)
Source Setup:	src hash (SHA256): < F61ADE21982F803F64D2CEA2C9CA90C23056CA852CCC515D17827038154E8C1E > src hash (SHA1): < 70CC62B43F6A41CA4D6760AA0B9B4C415D3F48E2 > src hash (MD5): < 746B4C06CDD5FBD67C0820DB4325B40C > 156301488 total sectors (80026361856 bytes) Model (ST380815AS) serial # (6QZ5C9V5) N Start LBA Length Start C/H/S End C/H/S boot Partition type 1 P 000000063 020971520 0000/001/01 1023/254/63 AF other 2 P 020971629 010485536 1023/254/63 1023/254/63 AF other 3 P 031457223 006291456 1023/254/63 1023/254/63 A8 other 4 X 037748679 008388694 1023/254/63 1023/254/63 05 extended 5 S 000000039 004194304 1023/254/63 1023/254/63 AF other 6 x 004194343 004194351 1023/254/63 1023/254/63 05 extended 7 S 000000047 004194304 1023/254/63 1023/254/63 AF other 8 S 000000000 000000000 0000/000/00 0000/000/00 00 empty entry 1 020971520 sectors 10737418240 bytes 2 010485536 sectors 5368594432 bytes 3 006291456 sectors 3221225472 bytes 5 004194304 sectors 2147483648 bytes 7 004194304 sectors 2147483648 bytes
Log Highlights:	====== Destination drive setup ====== 625142448 sectors wiped with 5D

====== Tool Settings: ====== image size: 4Gb image format: dd

OS: Linux ubuntu 2.6.32-33-generic #70-Ubuntu SMP Thu Jul 7 21:09:46 UTC 2011 i686 GNU/Linux

====== Image file segments ======   1 4000000000 2012-03-08 14:08 da-06-sata28.001   2   1708 2012-03-08 14:41 da-06-sata28.001.txt   3 4000000000 2012-03-08 14:09 da-06-sata28.002   . . .   20 4000000000 2012-03-08 14:28 da-06-sata28.020   21   26361856 2012-03-08 14:28 da-06-sata28.021   22   16384 2012-03-08 14:04 lost+found ======== Excerpt from Tool log ======== |

```
                  Case: da-06-sata28
                  Drive Geometry:
                   Cylinders: 9729
                   Heads: 255
                   Sectors per Track: 63
                   Bytes per Sector: 512
                   Sector Count: 156301488
                  Physical Drive Information:
                   Drive Model: ATA ST380815AS
                   Drive Interface Type: SCSI
                   Source data size: 76319 MB
                   Sector count:     156301488
                  Source hash:
                   MD5:    746b4c06cdd5fbd67c0820db4325b40c
                   SHA1:   70cc62b43f6a41ca4d6760aa0b9b4c415d3f48e2
                  Verification hash:
                   MD5:    746b4c06cdd5fbd67c0820db4325b40c
                   SHA1:   70cc62b43f6a41ca4d6760aa0b9b4c415d3f48e2
                  Segment list:
                    /media/xxx/da-06-sata28.001
                    /media/xxx/da-06-sata28.002
                    /media/xxx/da-06-sata28.003
                    /media/xxx/da-06-sata28.004
                    /media/xxx/da-06-sata28.005
                    /media/xxx/da-06-sata28.006
                    /media/xxx/da-06-sata28.007
                    /media/xxx/da-06-sata28.008
                    /media/xxx/da-06-sata28.009
                    /media/xxx/da-06-sata28.010
                    /media/xxx/da-06-sata28.011
                    /media/xxx/da-06-sata28.012
                    /media/xxx/da-06-sata28.013
                    /media/xxx/da-06-sata28.014
                    /media/xxx/da-06-sata28.015
                    /media/xxx/da-06-sata28.016
                    /media/xxx/da-06-sata28.017
                    /media/xxx/da-06-sata28.018
                    /media/xxx/da-06-sata28.019
                    /media/xxx/da-06-sata28.020
                    /media/xxx/da-06-sata28.021
                  ======== End of Excerpt from Tool log ========
```

Results:

Assertion & Expected Result	Actual Result
AM-01 Source acquired using interface AI.	as expected
AM-02 Source is type DS.	as expected
AM-03 Execution environment is XE.	as expected
AM-05 An image is created on file system type FS.	as expected
AM-06 All visible sectors acquired.	as expected
AM-08 All sectors accurately acquired.	as expected
AO-01 Image file is complete and accurate.	as expected
AO-05 Multifile image created.	as expected
AO-22 Tool calculates hashes by block.	option not available
AO-23 Logged information is correct.	as expected
AO-24 Source is unchanged by acquisition.	not checked

Analysis: Expected results achieved

5.2.19 DA-06-SATA48

Test Case DA-06-SATA48 AccessData FTK Imager CLI v2.9	
Case Summary:	DA-06 Acquire a physical device using access interface AI to an image file.
Assertions:	AM-01 The tool uses access interface SRC-AI to access the digital source.
	AM-02 The tool acquires digital source DS.
	AM-03 The tool executes in execution environment XE.
	AM-05 If image file creation is specified, the tool creates an image file on file system type FS.
	AM-06 All visible sectors are acquired from the digital source.
	AM-08 All sectors acquired from the digital source are acquired accurately.
	AO-01 If the tool creates an image file, the data represented by the image file is the same as the data acquired by the tool.
	AO-05 If the tool creates a multi-file image of a requested size then all the individual files shall be no larger than the requested size.
	AO-22 If requested, the tool calculates block hashes for a specified block size during an acquisition for each block acquired from the digital source.
	AO-23 If the tool logs any log significant information, the information is accurately recorded in the log file.
	AO-24 If the tool executes in a forensically safe execution environment, the digital source is unchanged by the acquisition process.
Tester Name:	csr
Test Host:	DeathStar
Test Date:	Fri Mar 9 16:22:14 2012
Drives:	src(16-SATA) dst (none) other (5D-SATA)
Source Setup:	src hash (SHA1): < F82982A9C63133988C1D2B4DA7C9C25CCA2D77A5 >
	src hash (MD5): < 7BB1D64D47671ED3E69130A2AD08FA02 >
	312581808 total sectors (160041885696 bytes)
	19456/254/63 (max cyl/hd values)
	19457/255/63 (number of cyl/hd)
	Model (WDC WD1600JD-00G) serial # (WD-WMAES2058252)
	N Start LBA Length Start C/H/S End C/H/S boot Partition type
	1 P 000000063 312560577 0000/001/01 1023/254/63 Boot 07 NTFS
	2 P 000000000 000000000 0000/000/00 0000/000/00 00 empty entry
	3 P 000000000 000000000 0000/000/00 0000/000/00 00 empty entry
	4 P 000000000 000000000 0000/000/00 0000/000/00 00 empty entry
	1 312560577 sectors 160031015424 bytes
Log Highlights:	====== Destination drive setup ======
	625142448 sectors wiped with 5D
	====== Tool Settings: ======
	size:3088112531 MB
	image format: e01
	OS: Linux ubuntu 2.6.32-33-generic #70-Ubuntu SMP Thu Jul 7 21:09:46 UTC 2011 i686 GNU/Linux
	====== Image file segments ======
	1 3088112531 2012-03-09 13:36 da-06-sata48.E01
	2 1116 2012-03-09 13:47 da-06-sata48.E01.txt
	3 16384 2012-03-08 14:04 lost+found
	======== Excerpt from Tool log ========
	Case: da-06-sata48
	Drive Geometry:
	Cylinders: 19457
	Heads: 255
	Sectors per Track: 63
	Bytes per Sector: 512
	Sector Count: 312581808
	Physical Drive Information:
	Drive Model: ATA WDC WD1600JD-00G
	Drive Interface Type: SCSI
	Source data size: 152627 MB
	Sector count: 312581808
	Source hash:

```
         MD5:     7bb1d64d47671ed3e69130a2ad08fa02
         SHA1:    f82982a9c63133988c1d2b4da7c9c25cca2d77a5
         Verification hash:
         MD5:     7bb1d64d47671ed3e69130a2ad08fa02
         SHA1:    f82982a9c63133988c1d2b4da7c9c25cca2d77a5
         Segment list:
          /media/xxx/da-06-sata48.E01
         ======== End of Excerpt from Tool log ========

         ====== Source drive rehash ======
         Rehash (SHA1) of source: F82982A9C63133988C1D2B4DA7C9C25CCA2D77A5
```

Results:	Assertion & Expected Result	Actual Result
	AM-01 Source acquired using interface AI.	as expected
	AM-02 Source is type DS.	as expected
	AM-03 Execution environment is XE.	as expected
	AM-05 An image is created on file system type FS.	as expected
	AM-06 All visible sectors acquired.	as expected
	AM-08 All sectors accurately acquired.	as expected
	AO-01 Image file is complete and accurate.	as expected
	AO-05 Multifile image created.	as expected
	AO-22 Tool calculates hashes by block.	option not available
	AO-23 Logged information is correct.	as expected
	AO-24 Source is unchanged by acquisition.	as expected

Analysis:	Expected results achieved

5.2.20   DA-06-SCSI

Test Case DA-06-SCSI AccessData FTK Imager CLI v2.9	
Case Summary:	DA-06 Acquire a physical device using access interface AI to an image file.
Assertions:	AM-01 The tool uses access interface SRC-AI to access the digital source. AM-02 The tool acquires digital source DS. AM-03 The tool executes in execution environment XE. AM-05 If image file creation is specified, the tool creates an image file on file system type FS. AM-06 All visible sectors are acquired from the digital source. AM-08 All sectors acquired from the digital source are acquired accurately. AO-01 If the tool creates an image file, the data represented by the image file is the same as the data acquired by the tool. AO-05 If the tool creates a multi-file image of a requested size then all the individual files shall be no larger than the requested size. AO-22 If requested, the tool calculates block hashes for a specified block size during an acquisition for each block acquired from the digital source. AO-23 If the tool logs any log significant information, the information is accurately recorded in the log file. AO-24 If the tool executes in a forensically safe execution environment, the digital source is unchanged by the acquisition process.
Tester Name:	csr
Test Host:	Frank
Test Date:	Wed Apr 18 13:40:12 2012
Drives:	src(E0) dst (none) other (AA)
Source Setup:	src hash (SHA1): < 4A6941F1337A8A22B10FC844B4D7FA6158BECB82 > src hash (MD5): < A97C8F36B7AC9D5233B90AC09284F938 > 17938985 total sectors (9184760320 bytes) Model (ATLAS10K2-TY092J) serial # (169028142436)

Log Highlights:	====== Destination drive setup ======
	60030432 sectors wiped with AA
	
	====== Tool Settings: ======
	image size: 9184760320 MB
	image format:dd
	
	OS: Linux ubuntu 2.6.32-33-generic #70-Ubuntu SMP Thu Jul 7 21:09:46 UTC 2011 i686 GNU/Linux
	
	====== Image file segments ======
	    1 9184760320 2012-04-19 14:55 da-14-scsi.001
	    2 1111 2012-04-19 15:00 da-14-scsi.001.txt
	    3 0 2012-04-19 15:01 ls.txt
	
	======== Excerpt from Tool log ========
	Case: da-06-scsi
	Drive Geometry:
	 Cylinders: 1116
	 Heads: 255
	 Sectors per Track: 63
	 Bytes per Sector: 512
	 Sector Count: 17938985
	Physical Drive Information:
	 Drive Model: QUANTUM ATLAS10K2-TY092J
	 Drive Interface Type: SCSI
	 Source data size: 8759 MB
	 Sector count: 17938985
	Source hash:
	 MD5: a97c8f36b7ac9d5233b90ac09284f938
	 SHA1: 4a6941f1337a8a22b10fc844b4d7fa6158becb82
	Verification hash:
	 MD5: a97c8f36b7ac9d5233b90ac09284f938
	 SHA1: 4a6941f1337a8a22b10fc844b4d7fa6158becb82
	Segment list:
	 /media/xxx/da-14-scsi.001

	======== End of Excerpt from Tool log ========
	====== Source drive rehash ======
	Rehash (SHA1) of source: 4A6941F1337A8A22B10FC844B4D7FA6158BECB82

Results:	

Assertion & Expected Result	Actual Result
AM-01 Source acquired using interface AI.	as expected
AM-02 Source is type DS.	as expected
AM-03 Execution environment is XE.	as expected
AM-05 An image is created on file system type FS.	as expected
AM-06 All visible sectors acquired.	as expected
AM-08 All sectors accurately acquired.	as expected
AO-01 Image file is complete and accurate.	as expected
AO-05 Multifile image created.	as expected
AO-22 Tool calculates hashes by block.	option not available
AO-23 Logged information is correct.	as expected
AO-24 Source is unchanged by acquisition.	as expected

Analysis:	Expected results achieved

5.2.21   DA-06-USB

Test Case DA-06-USB AccessData FTK Imager CLI v2.9	
Case Summary:	DA-06 Acquire a physical device using access interface AI to an image file.
Assertions:	AM-01 The tool uses access interface SRC-AI to access the digital source. AM-02 The tool acquires digital source DS. AM-03 The tool executes in execution environment XE. AM-05 If image file creation is specified, the tool creates an image file on file system type FS. AM-06 All visible sectors are acquired from the digital source. AM-08 All sectors acquired from the digital source are acquired accurately. AO-01 If the tool creates an image file, the data represented by the image file is the same as the data acquired by the tool. AO-05 If the tool creates a multi-file image of a requested size then all the individual files shall be no larger than the requested size. AO-22 If requested, the tool calculates block hashes for a specified block size during an acquisition for each block acquired from the digital source. AO-23 If the tool logs any log significant information, the information is accurately recorded in the log file. AO-24 If the tool executes in a forensically safe execution environment, the digital source is unchanged by the acquisition process.
Tester Name:	csr
Test Host:	DeathStar
Test Date:	Wed Jul 25 10:09:17 2012
Drives:	src(63-FU2) dst (none) other (5D-SATA)
Source Setup:	src hash (SHA256): < EC8EF011494BA6DA18F74C47547C3E74E7180585096A830F9247A98EF613BB1D > src hash (SHA1): < F7069EDCBEAC863C88DECED82159F22DA96BE99B > src hash (MD5): < EE217BC4FA4F3D1B4021D29B065AA9EC > 117304992 total sectors (60060155904 bytes) Model (SP0612N) serial # () N Start LBA Length Start C/H/S End C/H/S boot Partition type 1 P 000000063 004192902 0000/001/01 0260/254/63 Boot 06 Fat16 2 X 004192965 113097600 0261/000/01 1023/254/63 0F extended 3 S 000000063 113097537 0261/001/01 1023/254/63 0B Fat32 4 S 000000000 000000000 0000/000/00 0000/000/00 00 empty entry 5 P 000000000 000000000 0000/000/00 0000/000/00 00 empty entry 6 P 000000000 000000000 0000/000/00 0000/000/00 00 empty entry 1 004192902 sectors 2146765824 bytes 3 113097537 sectors 57905938944 bytes

Log Highlights:	====== Tool Settings: ======
	image size:887829024 MB
	image format: s01
	
	Write Block: 18 Tableau Forensic USB
	
	OS: Linux ubuntu 2.6.32-33-generic #70-Ubuntu SMP Thu Jul 7 21:09:46 UTC 2011 i686 GNU/Linux
	
	====== Image file segments ======
	    1 887829024 2012-07-25 14:17 da-06-usb.s01
	    2 1105 2012-07-25 14:27 logfile.txt
	    3 0 2012-07-25 15:53 ls.txt
	
	======== Excerpt from Tool log ========
	Case: da-06-usb
	Drive Geometry:
	 Cylinders: 7301
	 Heads: 255
	 Sectors per Track: 63
	 Bytes per Sector: 512
	 Sector Count: 117304992
	Physical Drive Information:
	 Drive Model: SAMSUNG SP0612N

Test Case DA-06-USB AccessData FTK Imager CLI v2.9

```
                  Drive Interface Type: SCSI
                  Source data size: 57277 MB
                  Sector count:    117304992
                  Source hash:
                   MD5:    ee217bc4fa4f3d1b4021d29b065aa9ec
                   SHA1:   f7069edcbeac863c88deced82159f22da96be99b
                  Verification hash:
                   MD5:    ee217bc4fa4f3d1b4021d29b065aa9ec
                   SHA1:   f7069edcbeac863c88deced82159f22da96be99b
                  Segment list:
                   /media/cftt/da-06-usb.s01
                  ======== End of Excerpt from Tool log ========
```

Results:		
	Assertion & Expected Result	**Actual Result**
	AM-01 Source acquired using interface AI.	as expected
	AM-02 Source is type DS.	as expected
	AM-03 Execution environment is XE.	as expected
	AM-05 An image is created on file system type FS.	as expected
	AM-06 All visible sectors acquired.	as expected
	AM-08 All sectors accurately acquired.	as expected
	AO-01 Image file is complete and accurate.	as expected
	AO-05 Multifile image created.	as expected
	AO-22 Tool calculates hashes by block.	option not available
	AO-23 Logged information is correct.	as expected
	AO-24 Source is unchanged by acquisition.	not checked

Analysis:	Expected results achieved

5.2.22 DA-07-CF

Test Case DA-07-CF AccessData FTK Imager CLI v2.9	
Case Summary:	DA-07 Acquire a digital source of type DS to an image file.
Assertions:	AM-01 The tool uses access interface SRC-AI to access the digital source. AM-02 The tool acquires digital source DS. AM-03 The tool executes in execution environment XE. AM-05 If image file creation is specified, the tool creates an image file on file system type FS. AM-06 All visible sectors are acquired from the digital source. AM-08 All sectors acquired from the digital source are acquired accurately. AO-01 If the tool creates an image file, the data represented by the image file is the same as the data acquired by the tool. AO-05 If the tool creates a multi-file image of a requested size then all the individual files shall be no larger than the requested size. AO-22 If requested, the tool calculates block hashes for a specified block size during an acquisition for each block acquired from the digital source. AO-23 If the tool logs any log significant information, the information is accurately recorded in the log file. AO-24 If the tool executes in a forensically safe execution environment, the digital source is unchanged by the acquisition process.
Tester Name:	csr
Test Host:	DeathStar
Test Date:	Mon Mar 26 08:52:36 2012
Drives:	src(C1-CF) dst (none) other (2A-SATA)

Source Setup:	src hash (SHA256): <
	C7CF0218222DF80D5316511D6814266C7FA507C13F795AD3D323BB73C1590D80 >
	src hash (SHA1): < 5B8235178DF99FA307430C088F81746606638A0B >
	src hash (MD5): < 776DF8B4D2589E21DEBCF589EDC16D78 >
	503808 total sectors (257949696 bytes)
	Model (CF) serial # ()
	  N Start LBA Length Start C/H/S End C/H/S boot Partition type
	  1 P 778135908 1141509631 0357/116/40 0357/032/45 Boot 72 other
	  2 P 168689522 1936028240 0288/115/43 0367/114/50 Boot 65 other
	  3 P 1869881465 1936028192 0366/032/33 0357/032/43 Boot 79 other
	  4 P 2885681152 000055499 0372/097/50 0000/010/00 Boot 0D other
	  1 1141509631 sectors 584452931072 bytes
	  2 1936028240 sectors 991246458880 bytes
	  3 1936028192 sectors 991246434304 bytes
	  4 000055499 sectors 28415488 bytes

Log Highlights:	====== Tool Settings: ======
	image size: 3835886 MB
	image format: e01
	
	Write Block: 7 UltraBlock Forensic Card Reader
	
	OS: Linux debian 2.6.32-5-486 #1 Mon Oct 3 03:34:28 UTC 2011 i686 GNU/Linux
	
	====== Image file segments ======
	    1 3835886 Mar 26 09:18 da-07-cf.E01
	    2 1097 Mar 26 09:18 da-07-cf.E01.txt
	    3 16384 Mar 26 09:03 lost+found
	
	======== Excerpt from Tool log ========
	Case: da-07-cf
	Drive Geometry:
	 Cylinders: 1015
	 Heads: 8
	 Sectors per Track: 62
	 Bytes per Sector: 512
	 Sector Count: 503808
	Physical Drive Information:
	 Drive Model: ICSI CF Card CF
	 Drive Interface Type: SCSI
	 Source data size: 246 MB

```
               Sector count:    503808
               Source hash:
                 MD5:    776df8b4d2589e21debcf589edc16d78
                 SHA1:   5b8235178df99fa307430c088f81746606638a0b
               Verification hash:
                 MD5:    776df8b4d2589e21debcf589edc16d78
                 SHA1:   5b8235178df99fa307430c088f81746606638a0b
               Segment list:
                 /media/xxx/da-07-cf.E01
               ======== End of Excerpt from Tool log ========
```

Results:		
	Assertion & Expected Result	**Actual Result**
	AM-01 Source acquired using interface AI.	as expected
	AM-02 Source is type DS.	as expected
	AM-03 Execution environment is XE.	as expected
	AM-05 An image is created on file system type FS.	as expected
	AM-06 All visible sectors acquired.	as expected
	AM-08 All sectors accurately acquired.	as expected
	AO-01 Image file is complete and accurate.	as expected
	AO-05 Multifile image created.	as expected
	AO-22 Tool calculates hashes by block.	option not available
	AO-23 Logged information is correct.	as expected
	AO-24 Source is unchanged by acquisition.	not checked

Analysis:	Expected results achieved

5.2.23 DA-07-EXT3

Test Case DA-07-EXT3 AccessData FTK Imager CLI v2.9	
Case Summary:	DA-07 Acquire a digital source of type DS to an image file.
Assertions:	AM-01 The tool uses access interface SRC-AI to access the digital source. AM-02 The tool acquires digital source DS. AM-03 The tool executes in execution environment XE. AM-05 If image file creation is specified, the tool creates an image file on file system type FS. AM-06 All visible sectors are acquired from the digital source. AM-08 All sectors acquired from the digital source are acquired accurately. AO-01 If the tool creates an image file, the data represented by the image file is the same as the data acquired by the tool. AO-05 If the tool creates a multi-file image of a requested size then all the individual files shall be no larger than the requested size. AO-22 If requested, the tool calculates block hashes for a specified block size during an acquisition for each block acquired from the digital source. AO-23 If the tool logs any log significant information, the information is accurately recorded in the log file. AO-24 If the tool executes in a forensically safe execution environment, the digital source is unchanged by the acquisition process.
Tester Name:	csr
Test Host:	DeathStar
Test Date:	Tue Apr 17 13:10:27 2012
Drives:	src(49-SATA) dst (none) other (1E-LAP)
Source Setup:	src hash (SHA1): < 6EC98F42EB5914D1F9D1661C0BB0A3660569F95B > src hash (MD5): < 30BAB74F67783C0555BCBD73DD4D0D5E > 156301488 total sectors (80026361856 bytes) Model (ST380815AS) serial # (5QZ5TD8Y) N Start LBA Length Start C/H/S End C/H/S boot Partition type 1 P 000002048 010485760 0000/032/33 0652/213/09 07 NTFS 2 P 010490445 005863725 0653/000/01 1017/254/63 83 Linux 3 P 016354170 007807590 1018/000/01 1023/254/63 83 Linux 4 P 000000000 000000000 0000/000/00 0000/000/00 00 empty entry 1 010485760 sectors 5368709120 bytes 2 005863725 sectors 3002227200 bytes 3 007807590 sectors 3997486080 bytes 49-SATAEXT3-md5sum 5863725 A25176AE775F65181DAC8C8D051DDF5D 49-SATAEXT3-sha1sum 5863725 FDF0F2BA2D4CB2D45E45717213AE218880236418

Log Highlights:	====== Destination drive setup ======
	
	====== Tool Settings: ======
	image size: 3002227200 MB
	image format: dd
	
	  Write Block: 11 TABLEAU SATA Bridge
	
	  OS: Linux debian 2.6.32-5-486 #1 Mon Oct 3 03:34:28 UTC 2011 i686 GNU/Linux
	
	  ====== Image file segments ======
	    1 3002227200 Apr 17 14:51 da-07-ext3.001
	    2 849 Apr 17 14:51 logfile.txt
	    3 0 Apr 17 14:52 ls.txt
	
	  ======== Excerpt from Tool log ========
	Case: da-07-ext3
	Drive Geometry:
	Physical Drive Information:
	  Source data size: 2863 MB
	  Sector count: 5863725
	Source hash:
	  MD5: a25176ae775f65181dac8c8d051ddf5d
	  SHA1: fdf0f2ba2d4cb2d45e45717213ae218880236418
	Verification hash:
	  MD5: a25176ae775f65181dac8c8d051ddf5d
	  SHA1: fdf0f2ba2d4cb2d45e45717213ae218880236418

Test Case DA-07-EXT3 AccessData FTK Imager CLI v2.9	
	Segment list: /media/xxx/da-07-ext3.001 ======== End of Excerpt from Tool log ========
Results:	

Assertion & Expected Result	Actual Result
AM-01 Source acquired using interface AI.	as expected
AM-02 Source is type DS.	as expected
AM-03 Execution environment is XE.	as expected
AM-05 An image is created on file system type FS.	as expected
AM-06 All visible sectors acquired.	as expected
AM-08 All sectors accurately acquired.	as expected
AO-01 Image file is complete and accurate.	as expected
AO-05 Multifile image created.	as expected
AO-22 Tool calculates hashes by block.	option not available
AO-23 Logged information is correct.	as expected
AO-24 Source is unchanged by acquisition.	not checked

Analysis:	Expected results achieved

5.2.24   DA-07-EXT4

Test Case DA-07-EXT4 AccessData FTK Imager CLI v2.9	
Case Summary:	DA-07 Acquire a digital source of type DS to an image file.
Assertions:	AM-01 The tool uses access interface SRC-AI to access the digital source. AM-02 The tool acquires digital source DS. AM-03 The tool executes in execution environment XE. AM-05 If image file creation is specified, the tool creates an image file on file system type FS. AM-06 All visible sectors are acquired from the digital source. AM-08 All sectors acquired from the digital source are acquired accurately. AO-01 If the tool creates an image file, the data represented by the image file is the same as the data acquired by the tool. AO-05 If the tool creates a multi-file image of a requested size then all the individual files shall be no larger than the requested size. AO-22 If requested, the tool calculates block hashes for a specified block size during an acquisition for each block acquired from the digital source. AO-23 If the tool logs any log significant information, the information is accurately recorded in the log file. AO-24 If the tool executes in a forensically safe execution environment, the digital source is unchanged by the acquisition process.
Tester Name:	csr
Test Host:	DeathStar
Test Date:	Tue Apr 17 15:06:27 2012
Drives:	src(49-SATA) dst (none) other (1E-LAP)
Source Setup:	src hash (SHA1): < 6EC98F42EB5914D1F9D1661C0BB0A3660569F95B > src hash (MD5): < 30BAB74F67783C0555BCBD73DD4D0D5E > 156301488 total sectors (80026361856 bytes) Model (ST380815AS) serial # (5QZ5TD8Y) N Start LBA Length Start C/H/S End C/H/S boot Partition type 1 P 000002048 010485760 0000/032/33 0652/213/09 07 NTFS 2 P 010490445 005863725 0653/000/01 1017/254/63 83 Linux 3 P 016354170 007807590 1018/000/01 1023/254/63 83 Linux 4 P 000000000 000000000 0000/000/00 0000/000/00 00 empty entry 1 010485760 sectors 5368709120 bytes 2 005863725 sectors 3002227200 bytes 3 007807590 sectors 3997486080 bytes 49-SATAEXT4-md5sum 7807590 567F2826AB468D69F97CB0D1878BE25D 49-SATAEXT4-sha1sum 7807590 F28A79F5E5CD28F859A1AC6B18A2CA3682D15A2A

Log Highlights:	====== Destination drive setup ======
	
	====== Tool Settings: ======
	image file: dd
	image size: 3997486080 MB
	
	Write Block: 11 TABLEAU SATA Bridge
	
	OS: Linux debian 2.6.32-5-486 #1 Mon Oct 3 03:34:28 UTC 2011 i686 GNU/Linux
	
	====== Image file segments ======
	   1 3002227200 Apr 17 14:51 da-07-ext3.001
	   2 3997486080 Apr 17 14:58 da-07-ext4.001
	   3 849 Apr 17 14:59 logfile.txt
	   4 0 Apr 17 15:00 ls.txt
	
	======== Excerpt from Tool log ========
	Case: da-07-ext4
	Drive Geometry:
	Physical Drive Information:
	 Source data size: 3812 MB
	 Sector count: 7807590
	Source hash:
	 MD5: 567f2826ab468d69f97cb0d1878be25d
	 SHA1: f28a79f5e5cd28f859a1ac6b18a2ca3682d15a2a
	Verification hash:
	 MD5: 567f2826ab468d69f97cb0d1878be25d

Test Case DA-07-EXT4 AccessData FTK Imager CLI v2.9	
	SHA1: f28a79f5e5cd28f859a1ac6b18a2ca3682d15a2a Segment list: /media/xxx/da-07-ext4.001 ======== End of Excerpt from Tool log ========

Results:

Assertion & Expected Result	Actual Result
AM-01 Source acquired using interface AI.	as expected
AM-02 Source is type DS.	as expected
AM-03 Execution environment is XE.	as expected
AM-05 An image is created on file system type FS.	as expected
AM-06 All visible sectors acquired.	as expected
AM-08 All sectors accurately acquired.	as expected
AO-01 Image file is complete and accurate.	as expected
AO-05 Multifile image created.	as expected
AO-22 Tool calculates hashes by block.	option not available
AO-23 Logged information is correct.	as expected
AO-24 Source is unchanged by acquisition.	not checked

Analysis: Expected results achieved

5.2.25   DA-07-F16

Test Case DA-07-F16 AccessData FTK Imager CLI v2.9	
Case Summary:	DA-07 Acquire a digital source of type DS to an image file.
Assertions:	AM-01 The tool uses access interface SRC-AI to access the digital source. AM-02 The tool acquires digital source DS. AM-03 The tool executes in execution environment XE. AM-05 If image file creation is specified, the tool creates an image file on file system type FS. AM-06 All visible sectors are acquired from the digital source. AM-08 All sectors acquired from the digital source are acquired accurately. AO-01 If the tool creates an image file, the data represented by the image file is the same as the data acquired by the tool. AO-05 If the tool creates a multi-file image of a requested size then all the individual files shall be no larger than the requested size. AO-22 If requested, the tool calculates block hashes for a specified block size during an acquisition for each block acquired from the digital source. AO-23 If the tool logs any log significant information, the information is accurately recorded in the log file. AO-24 If the tool executes in a forensically safe execution environment, the digital source is unchanged by the acquisition process.
Tester Name:	csr
Test Host:	DeathStar
Test Date:	Thu Mar 22 15:24:01 2012
Drives:	src(01-IDE) dst (none) other (32-SATA)
Source Setup:	src hash (SHA1): < A48BB5665D6DC57C22DB68E2F723DA9AA8DF82B9 > src hash (MD5): < F458F673894753FA6A0EC8B8EC63848E > 78165360 total sectors (40020664320 bytes) Model (0BB-00JHC0) serial # (WD-WMAMC74171) N Start LBA Length Start C/H/S End C/H/S boot Partition type 1 P 000000063 020980827 0000/001/01 1023/254/63 0C Fat32X 2 X 020980890 057175335 1023/000/01 1023/254/63 0F extended 3 S 000000063 000032067 1023/001/01 1023/254/63 01 Fat12 4 x 000032130 002104515 1023/000/01 1023/254/63 05 extended 5 S 000000063 002104452 1023/001/01 1023/254/63 06 Fat16 6 x 002136645 004192965 1023/000/01 1023/254/63 05 extended 7 S 000000063 004192902 1023/001/01 1023/254/63 16 other 8 x 006329610 008401995 1023/000/01 1023/254/63 05 extended 9 S 000000063 008401932 1023/001/01 1023/254/63 0B Fat32 10 x 014731605 010490445 1023/000/01 1023/254/63 05 extended 11 S 000000063 010490382 1023/001/01 1023/254/63 03 Linux 12 x 025222050 004209030 1023/000/01 1023/254/63 05 extended 13 S 000000063 004208967 1023/001/01 1023/254/63 82 Linux swap 14 x 029431080 027744255 1023/000/01 1023/254/63 05 extended 15 S 000000063 027744192 1023/001/01 1023/254/63 07 NTFS 16 S 000000000 000000000 0000/000/00 0000/000/00 00 empty entry 17 P 000000000 000000000 0000/000/00 0000/000/00 00 empty entry 18 P 000000000 000000000 0000/000/00 0000/000/00 00 empty entry 1 020980827 sectors 10742183424 bytes 3 000032067 sectors 16418304 bytes 5 002104452 sectors 1077479424 bytes 7 004192902 sectors 2146765824 bytes 9 008401932 sectors 4301789184 bytes 11 010490382 sectors 5371075584 bytes 13 004208967 sectors 2154991104 bytes 15 027744192 sectors 14205026304 bytes 01F16-md5 1077479423 8B24F3D793188AF2473F69B267AFDA42 01F16-sha1 1077479423 074BA831B10132F4BF9F86AFAB37CB7FEF482C7D
Log Highlights:	====== Tool Settings: ====== image size: 15999505 MB image format: s01 Write Block: 3 FASTBloc IDE OS: Linux debian 2.6.32-5-486 #1 Mon Oct 3 03:34:28 UTC 2011 i686 GNU/Linux

```
====== Image file segments ======
      1  15999505 Mar 23 07:31 da-07-F16.s01
      2       847 Mar 23 07:31 da-07-F16.s01.txt
      3         0 Mar 23 07:32 ls.txt

======== Excerpt from Tool log ========
Case: da-07-f16
Drive Geometry:
Physical Drive Information:
 Source data size: 1027 MB
 Sector count:    2104452
Source hash:
 MD5:    8b24f3d793188af2473f69b267afda42
 SHA1:   074ba831b10132f4bf9f86afab37cb7fef482c7d
Verification hash:
 MD5:    8b24f3d793188af2473f69b267afda42
 SHA1:   074ba831b10132f4bf9f86afab37cb7fef482c7d
Segment list:
 /media/xxx/da-07-F16.s01
======== End of Excerpt from Tool log ========
```

Results:

Assertion & Expected Result	Actual Result
AM-01 Source acquired using interface AI.	as expected
AM-02 Source is type DS.	as expected
AM-03 Execution environment is XE.	as expected
AM-05 An image is created on file system type FS.	as expected
AM-06 All visible sectors acquired.	as expected
AM-08 All sectors accurately acquired.	as expected
AO-01 Image file is complete and accurate.	as expected
AO-05 Multifile image created.	as expected
AO-22 Tool calculates hashes by block.	option not available
AO-23 Logged information is correct.	as expected
AO-24 Source is unchanged by acquisition.	not checked

Analysis: Expected results achieved

5.2.26   DA-07-F32

Test Case DA-07-F32 AccessData FTK Imager CLI v2.9	
Case Summary:	DA-07 Acquire a digital source of type DS to an image file.
Assertions:	AM-01 The tool uses access interface SRC-AI to access the digital source. AM-02 The tool acquires digital source DS. AM-03 The tool executes in execution environment XE. AM-05 If image file creation is specified, the tool creates an image file on file system type FS. AM-06 All visible sectors are acquired from the digital source. AM-08 All sectors acquired from the digital source are acquired accurately. AO-01 If the tool creates an image file, the data represented by the image file is the same as the data acquired by the tool. AO-05 If the tool creates a multi-file image of a requested size then all the individual files shall be no larger than the requested size. AO-22 If requested, the tool calculates block hashes for a specified block size during an acquisition for each block acquired from the digital source. AO-23 If the tool logs any log significant information, the information is accurately recorded in the log file. AO-24 If the tool executes in a forensically safe execution environment, the digital source is unchanged by the acquisition process.
Tester Name:	csr
Test Host:	DeathStar
Test Date:	Thu Mar 22 15:24:01 2012
Drives:	src(01-IDE) dst (none) other (32-SATA)

Source Setup:	src hash (SHA1): < A48BB5665D6DC57C22DB68E2F723DA9AA8DF82B9 >
	src hash (MD5): < F458F673894753FA6A0EC8B8EC63848E >
	78165360 total sectors (40020664320 bytes)
	Model (0BB-00JHC0) serial # (WD-WMAMC74171)
	<pre>N Start LBA Length Start C/H/S End C/H/S boot Partition type
	 1 P 000000063 020980827 0000/001/01 1023/254/63 0C Fat32X
	 2 X 020980890 057175335 1023/000/01 1023/254/63 0F extended
	 3 S 000000063 000032067 1023/001/01 1023/254/63 01 Fat12
	 4 x 000032130 002104515 1023/000/01 1023/254/63 05 extended
	 5 S 000000063 002104452 1023/001/01 1023/254/63 06 Fat16
	 6 x 002136645 004192965 1023/000/01 1023/254/63 05 extended
	 7 S 000000063 004192902 1023/001/01 1023/254/63 16 other
	 8 x 006329610 008401995 1023/000/01 1023/254/63 05 extended
	 9 S 000000063 008401932 1023/001/01 1023/254/63 0B Fat32
	10 x 014731605 010490445 1023/000/01 1023/254/63 05 extended
	11 S 000000063 010490382 1023/001/01 1023/254/63 83 Linux
	12 x 025222050 004209030 1023/000/01 1023/254/63 05 extended
	13 S 000000063 004208967 1023/001/01 1023/254/63 82 Linux swap
	14 x 029431080 027744255 1023/000/01 1023/254/63 05 extended
	15 S 000000063 027744192 1023/001/01 1023/254/63 07 NTFS
	16 S 000000000 000000000 0000/000/00 0000/000/00 00 empty entry
	17 P 000000000 000000000 0000/000/00 0000/000/00 00 empty entry
	18 P 000000000 000000000 0000/000/00 0000/000/00 00 empty entry</pre>1 020980827 sectors 10742183424 bytes
	3 000032067 sectors 16418304 bytes
	5 002104452 sectors 1077479424 bytes
	7 004192902 sectors 2146765824 bytes
	9 008401932 sectors 4301789184 bytes
	11 010490382 sectors 5371075584 bytes
	13 004208967 sectors 2154991104 bytes
	15 027744192 sectors 14205026304 bytes
	01F32-md5 4301789183 BFF7DC64C54339DA2A9D7972C076B514
	01F32-sha1 4301789183 B861D9E999F39750B484FFB693FF69DEC090C6B8
	01F32-sha256 4301789183
	CAE3A4CC33D59548063255D2AA4016940AC712DD96985AD9B94FF271CC3E943E

Log Highlights:	====== Tool Settings: ====== image size: 64081534 MB image format: e01

```
Write Block: 3 FASTBloc IDE

OS: Linux debian 2.6.32-5-486 #1 Mon Oct 3 03:34:28 UTC 2011 i686 GNU/Linux

====== Image file segments ======
    1 64081534 Mar 22 12:43 da-07-F32.E01
    2      847 Mar 22 12:43 da-07-F32.E01.txt
    3        0 Mar 22 12:43 ls.txt

======== Excerpt from Tool log ========
Case: da-07-f32
Drive Geometry:
Physical Drive Information:
 Source data size: 4102 MB
 Sector count:    8401932
Source hash:
 MD5:   bff7dc64c54339da2a9d7972c076b514
 SHA1:  b861d9e999f39750b484ffb693ff69dec090c6b8
Verification hash:
 MD5:   bff7dc64c54339da2a9d7972c076b514
 SHA1:  b861d9e999f39750b484ffb693ff69dec090c6b8
Segment list:
 /media/xxx/da-07-F32.E01
======== End of Excerpt from Tool log ========
```

Results:	

Assertion & Expected Result	Actual Result
AM-01 Source acquired using interface AI.	as expected
AM-02 Source is type DS.	as expected
AM-03 Execution environment is XE.	as expected
AM-05 An image is created on file system type FS.	as expected
AM-06 All visible sectors acquired.	as expected
AM-08 All sectors accurately acquired.	as expected
AO-01 Image file is complete and accurate.	as expected
AO-05 Multifile image created.	as expected
AO-22 Tool calculates hashes by block.	option not available
AO-23 Logged information is correct.	as expected
AO-24 Source is unchanged by acquisition.	not checked

Analysis:	Expected results achieved

5.2.27   DA-07-NT

Test Case DA-07-NT AccessData FTK Imager CLI v2.9	
Case Summary:	DA-07 Acquire a digital source of type DS to an image file.
Assertions:	AM-01 The tool uses access interface SRC-AI to access the digital source. AM-02 The tool acquires digital source DS. AM-03 The tool executes in execution environment XE. AM-05 If image file creation is specified, the tool creates an image file on file system type FS. AM-06 All visible sectors are acquired from the digital source. AM-08 All sectors acquired from the digital source are acquired accurately. AO-01 If the tool creates an image file, the data represented by the image file is the same as the data acquired by the tool. AO-05 If the tool creates a multi-file image of a requested size then all the individual files shall be no larger than the requested size. AO-22 If requested, the tool calculates block hashes for a specified block size during an acquisition for each block acquired from the digital source. AO-23 If the tool logs any log significant information, the information is accurately recorded in the log file. AO-24 If the tool executes in a forensically safe execution environment, the digital source is unchanged by the acquisition process.
Tester Name:	csr
Test Host:	DeathStar
Test Date:	Thu Mar 22 15:24:01 2012
Drives:	src(01-IDE) dst (none) other (32-SATA)

Source Setup:	src hash (SHA1): < A48BB5665D6DC57C22DB68E2F723DA9AA8DF82B9 >
	src hash (MD5): < F458F673894753FA6A0EC8B8EC63848E >
	78165360 total sectors (40020664320 bytes)
	Model (0BB-00JHC0) serial # (WD-WMAMC74171)
	<pre>N Start LBA Length Start C/H/S End C/H/S boot Partition type
	 1 P 000000063 020980827 0000/001/01 1023/254/63 0C Fat32X
	 2 X 020980890 057175335 1023/000/01 1023/254/63 0F extended
	 3 S 000000063 000032067 1023/001/01 1023/254/63 01 Fat12
	 4 x 000032130 002104515 1023/000/01 1023/254/63 05 extended
	 5 S 000000063 002104452 1023/001/01 1023/254/63 06 Fat16
	 6 x 002136645 004192965 1023/000/01 1023/254/63 05 extended
	 7 S 000000063 004192902 1023/001/01 1023/254/63 16 other
	 8 x 006329610 008401995 1023/000/01 1023/254/63 05 extended
	 9 S 000000063 008401932 1023/001/01 1023/254/63 0B Fat32
	10 x 014731605 010490445 1023/000/01 1023/254/63 05 extended
	11 S 000000063 010490382 1023/001/01 1023/254/63 03 Linux
	12 x 025222050 004209030 1023/000/01 1023/254/63 05 extended
	13 S 000000063 004208967 1023/001/01 1023/254/63 82 Linux swap
	14 x 029431080 027744255 1023/000/01 1023/254/63 05 extended
	15 S 000000063 027744192 1023/001/01 1023/254/63 07 NTFS
	16 S 000000000 000000000 0000/000/00 0000/000/00 00 empty entry
	17 P 000000000 000000000 0000/000/00 0000/000/00 00 empty entry
	18 P 000000000 000000000 0000/000/00 0000/000/00 00 empty entry
	 1 020980827 sectors 10742183424 bytes
	 3 000032067 sectors 16418304 bytes
	 5 002104452 sectors 1077479424 bytes
	 7 004192902 sectors 2146765824 bytes
	 9 008401932 sectors 4301789184 bytes
	11 010490382 sectors 5371075584 bytes
	13 004208967 sectors 2154991104 bytes
	15 027744192 sectors 14205026304 bytes</pre>01NT-md5 14205026303 92B27B30BEE8B0FFBA8C660FA1590D49
	01NT-sha1 14205026303 0FBA4C36295CB9622CD815577429C3A588C34D09

Log Highlights:	====== Tool Settings: ====== image size: 14205026304 MB image format: dd Write Block: 3 FASTBloc IDE OS: Linux debian 2.6.32-5-486 #1 Mon Oct 3 03:34:28 UTC 2011 i686 GNU/Linux

```
====== Image file segments ======
    1 14205026304 2012-03-23 14:19 da-07-NT.001
    2          847 2012-03-23 14:22 da-07-NT.001.txt

======== Excerpt from Tool log ========
Case: da-07-nt
Drive Geometry:
Physical Drive Information:
  Source data size: 13546 MB
  Sector count:    27744192
Source hash:
  MD5:    92b27b30bee8b0ffba8c660fa1590d49
  SHA1:   0fba4c36295cb9622cd815577429c3a588c34d09
Verification hash:
  MD5:    92b27b30bee8b0ffba8c660fa1590d49
  SHA1:   0fba4c36295cb9622cd815577429c3a588c34d09
Segment list:
  /media/xxx/da-07-NT.001
======== End of Excerpt from Tool log ========
```

	Assertion & Expected Result	Actual Result
Results:		
	AM-01 Source acquired using interface AI.	as expected
	AM-02 Source is type DS.	as expected
	AM-03 Execution environment is XE.	as expected
	AM-05 An image is created on file system type FS.	as expected
	AM-06 All visible sectors acquired.	as expected
	AM-08 All sectors accurately acquired.	as expected
	AO-01 Image file is complete and accurate.	as expected
	AO-05 Multifile image created.	as expected
	AO-22 Tool calculates hashes by block.	option not available
	AO-23 Logged information is correct.	as expected
	AO-24 Source is unchanged by acquisition.	not checked
Analysis:	Expected results achieved	

5.2.28   DA-07-THUMB

Test Case DA-07-THUMB AccessData FTK Imager CLI v2.9	
Case Summary:	DA-07 Acquire a digital source of type DS to an image file.
Assertions:	AM-01 The tool uses access interface SRC-AI to access the digital source. AM-02 The tool acquires digital source DS. AM-03 The tool executes in execution environment XE. AM-05 If image file creation is specified, the tool creates an image file on file system type FS. AM-06 All visible sectors are acquired from the digital source. AM-08 All sectors acquired from the digital source are acquired accurately. AO-01 If the tool creates an image file, the data represented by the image file is the same as the data acquired by the tool. AO-05 If the tool creates a multi-file image of a requested size then all the individual files shall be no larger than the requested size. AO-22 If requested, the tool calculates block hashes for a specified block size during an acquisition for each block acquired from the digital source. AO-23 If the tool logs any log significant information, the information is accurately recorded in the log file. AO-24 If the tool executes in a forensically safe execution environment, the digital source is unchanged by the acquisition process.
Tester Name:	csr
Test Host:	DeathStar
Test Date:	Mon Mar 26 10:07:46 2012
Drives:	src(D5-Thumb) dst (none) other (2A-SATA)
Source Setup:	src hash (SHA1): < D68520EF74A336E49DCCF83815B7B08FDC53E38A > src hash (MD5): < C843593624B2B3B878596D8760B19954 > 505856 total sectors (258998272 bytes) Model (usb2.0Flash Disk) serial # ()

Log Highlights:	====== Tool Settings: ======
	image format: s01
	image size:3853920 MB
	
	Write Block: 18 UltraBlock USB
	
	OS: Linux debian 2.6.32-5-486 #1 Mon Oct 3 03:34:28 UTC 2011 i686 GNU/Linux
	
	====== Image file segments ======
	    1 3853920 2012-03-26 10:17 da-07-thumb.s01
	    2 1106 2012-03-26 10:17 da-07-thumb.s01.txt
	
	======== Excerpt from Tool log ========
	Case: da-07-thumb
	Drive Geometry:
	 Cylinders: 1019
	 Heads: 8
	 Sectors per Track: 62
	 Bytes per Sector: 512
	 Sector Count: 505856
	Physical Drive Information:
	 Drive Model: CRUCIAL usb2.0Flash Disk
	 Drive Interface Type: SCSI
	 Source data size: 247 MB
	 Sector count: 505856
	Source hash:
	 MD5: c843593624b2b3b878596d8760b19954
	 SHA1: d68520ef74a336e49dccf83815b7b08fdc53e38a
	Verification hash:
	 MD5: c843593624b2b3b878596d8760b19954
	 SHA1: d68520ef74a336e49dccf83815b7b08fdc53e38a
	Segment list:
	  /media/xxx/da-07-thumb.s01
	======== End of Excerpt from Tool log ========

Results:	

Test Case DA-07-THUMB AccessData FTK Imager CLI v2.9		
	Assertion & Expected Result	**Actual Result**
	AM-01 Source acquired using interface AI.	as expected
	AM-02 Source is type DS.	as expected
	AM-03 Execution environment is XE.	as expected
	AM-05 An image is created on file system type FS.	as expected
	AM-06 All visible sectors acquired.	as expected
	AM-08 All sectors accurately acquired.	as expected
	AO-01 Image file is complete and accurate.	as expected
	AO-05 Multifile image created.	as expected
	AO-22 Tool calculates hashes by block.	option not available
	AO-23 Logged information is correct.	as expected
	AO-24 Source is unchanged by acquisition.	not checked
Analysis:	Expected results achieved	

5.2.29   DA-09

Test Case DA-09 AccessData FTK Imager CLI v2.9	
Case Summary:	DA-09 Acquire a digital source that has at least one faulty data sector.
Assertions:	AM-01 The tool uses access interface SRC-AI to access the digital source.
	AM-02 The tool acquires digital source DS.
	AM-03 The tool executes in execution environment XE.
	AM-05 If image file creation is specified, the tool creates an image file on file system type FS.
	AM-06 All visible sectors are acquired from the digital source.
	AM-08 All sectors acquired from the digital source are acquired accurately.
	AM-09 If unresolved errors occur while reading from the selected digital source, the tool notifies the user of the error type and location within the digital source.
	AM-10 If unresolved errors occur while reading from the selected digital source, the tool uses a benign fill in the destination object in place of the inaccessible data.
	AO-01 If the tool creates an image file, the data represented by the image file is the same as the data acquired by the tool.
	AO-05 If the tool creates a multi-file image of a requested size then all the individual files shall be no larger than the requested size.
	AO-22 If requested, the tool calculates block hashes for a specified block size during an acquisition for each block acquired from the digital source.
	AO-23 If the tool logs any log significant information, the information is accurately recorded in the log file.
	AO-24 If the tool executes in a forensically safe execution environment, the digital source is unchanged by the acquisition process.
Tester Name:	csr
Test Host:	DeathStar
Test Date:	Mon Mar 19 14:49:29 2012
Drives:	src(ED-BAD-CPR2) dst (4C-SATA) other (none)
Source Setup:	No before hash for ED-BAD-CPR2
	Known Bad Sector List for ED-CPR-BAD-2
	Manufacturer: Maxtor
	Model: DiamondMax Plus 9
	Serial Number: Y22HJL7C
	Capacity: 60GB
	Interface: SATA
	468 faulty sectors
	1344585, 2594747, 2595500, 2599086, 2599839, 2809909,
	2809910, 3422895, 3422896, 4116750, 4120336, 4120337,
	4121089, 4121090, 4696046, 4698397, 4703710, 4707186,
	4708105, 4711580, 4712499, 4714850, 4715770, 4719245,
	4723639, 4723640, 4724558, 4724559, 4728034, 4728953,
	4731304, 4732223, 4735699, 4740093, 4741012, 4743363,
	4745407, 4748677, 4752152, 4756547, 4757466, 4759817,
	4761860, 4761861, 4764211, 4764212, 4765130, 4765131,
	4768606, 4769525, 4773001, 4773920, 4776271, 4777190,
	4780665, 4781584, 5446946, 5448990, 5451341, 5452260,
	5620120, 5623595, 5623596, 5623597, 5624514, 5624515,
	5624516, 5626865, 5626866, 5626867, 5628909, 5631260,
	5632179, 5635655, 5636574, 5640049, 6021518, 6023869,
	6024788, 6028263, 7662307, 8340091, 8340092, 12178157,
	12179060, 12181370, 12182273, 12185687, 12186590, 12340277,
	13016906, 13049575, 13050477, 13050478, 14000022, 14000762,
	14004285, 14041240, 17135988, 17723611, 17876726, 18161032,
	18760155, 20090856, 20094289, 20095011, 20661414, 21693295,
	21694174, 21697502, 22730717, 22838734, 22838735, 24596104,
	24596105, 24596106, 26791779, 27686030, 28080041, 28081995,
	29555383, 29655054, 30488210, 30488211, 32215323, 32218669,
	33523139, 33991449, 35267814, 37975363, 38134596, 38136734,
	38137571, 38137572, 38207258, 38207259, 38542983, 38567425,
	38568109, 39421072, 39421909, 39425071, 40273501, 42836488,
	42837172, 42843548, 42847497, 42851446, 42854557, 43505180,

```
43508342, 43872574, 43873411, 45217120, 45217121, 45777316,
46221189, 46296219, 46296220, 46528674, 46955925, 47093653,
48537000, 48537662, 49911188, 49911189, 51017721, 51769307,
51769969, 51994516, 51994517, 53855354, 55793018, 55793019,
57316559, 57320313, 60571670, 60571671, 60571672, 60952349,
60952350, 60952993, 61535962, 61535963, 61535964, 62592910,
62593672, 62596563, 62597325, 62600215, 63140751, 63140752,
63141513, 63141514, 63144404, 63226363, 63229253, 63670246,
63972517, 63975497, 65576815, 65925948, 66146215, 67860503,
67860504, 68711104, 69100751, 69176705, 69189596, 69189597,
69189598, 69190358, 69190359, 69190360, 69974439, 69975201,
70656792, 72217315, 72801392, 72992581, 72992582, 73626901,
73626902, 75004819, 78164515, 78167178, 78167885, 78307369,
78415033, 78415034, 78693137, 79145838, 79146544, 79146545,
79146546, 79744714, 79745420, 79748084, 79748790, 79901007,
80691204, 80691205, 82083870, 82083871, 82083872, 83739051,
83739052, 84411502, 84553520, 85181194, 85418740, 87197252,
88020545, 88020546, 88021216, 88023752, 88024422, 88071013,
88071014, 88755730, 89294003, 92741348, 92741349, 92743744,
92743745, 94017998, 95929572, 95929573, 97369221, 97485310,
99685572, 100687317, 100689593, 102205339, 103403045,
104768238, 105074641, 105638643, 106115226, 106115791,
106117947, 106118512, 106120668, 106121233, 106122698,
106123954, 106123955, 106125419, 106125420, 106125984,
106125985, 106128141, 106128706, 106186051, 106936608,
107133037, 107276378, 108007258, 109270108, 109270673,
109272829, 109273394, 109275550, 109319902, 110072175,
111250371, 111251549, 111485059, 112587333, 112588682,
112588683, 112588684, 114286586, 114359887, 115110935,
116807008, 116807009, 116808918, 117175664, 117177512,
117178002, 117179850, 117180340, 117180341, 117181588,
117182678, 117182679, 117182680, 117183926, 117184417,
117186264, 117186265, 117106755, 117188602, 117188603,
117188604, 117189093, 117190341, 117193170, 117195017,
117195018, 117195508, 117197355, 117197356, 117197357,
117197846, 117199094, 117199584, 117201432, 117201922,
117201923, 117203770, 117204260, 117204261, 117204262,
117205508, 117206599, 117207846, 117207847, 117207848,
117208337, 117210185, 117210675, 117212523, 117213013,
117213014, 117214261, 117215352, 117217090, 117218938,
117219428, 117219429, 117221276, 117221766, 117221767,
117221768, 117223014, 117223505, 117225352, 117225353,
117225354, 117225843, 117227691, 117228181, 117229429,
117230519, 117230520, 117231767, 117232258, 117234105,
117234106, 117234596, 117236444, 117236934, 117238182,
117239272, 117239273, 117240520, 117241011, 117242858,
117242859, 117245687, 117245688, 117246935, 117247426,
117249273, 117249274, 117249764, 117251612, 117252102,
117253350, 117254440, 117254441, 117255688, 117256179,
117258026, 117258027, 117258517, 117260365, 117260855,
117262103, 117263193, 117263194, 117264441, 117264932,
117266779, 117266780, 117269270, 117269118, 117269608,
117270856, 117271946, 117271947, 117275533, 117276023,
117277871, 117278361, 117278362, 117278363, 117279609,
117280100, 117281947, 117281948, 117282438, 117284286,
117284776, 117286024, 117287114, 117287115, 117287116,
117288362, 117288853, 117290700, 117290701, 117290702,
117291191, 117293039, 117293529, 117294777, 117295867,
117295868, 117295869, 117297115, 117297606, 117299453,
117299454, 117299455, 119655644
```

Log Highlights:	====== Destination drive setup ====== 156301488 sectors wiped with 4C ====== Comparison of original to clone drive ====== Sectors compared: 120103200 Sectors match: 1344584 Sectors differ: 118758616 Bytes differ: 57716687376 Diffs range 1344584-120103199

```
Source (120103200) has 36198288 fewer sectors than destination (156301488)
Zero fill:              0
Src Byte fill (ED):     0
Dst Byte fill (4C): 36198288
Other fill:             0
Other no fill:          0
Zero fill range:
Src fill range:
Dst fill range:  120103200-156301487
Other fill range:
Other not filled range:
0 source read errors, 0 destination read errors

====== Tool Settings: ======
direct clone
```

Results:

Assertion & Expected Result	Actual Result
AM-01 Source acquired using interface AI.	as expected
AM-02 Source is type DS.	as expected
AM-03 Execution environment is XE.	as expected
AM-05 An image is created on file system type FS.	as expected
AM-06 All visible sectors acquired.	Some sectors skipped
AM-08 All sectors accurately acquired.	as expected
AM-09 Error logged.	No error reported
AM-10 Benign fill replaces inaccessible sectors.	as expected
AO-01 Image file is complete and accurate.	as expected
AO-05 Multifile image created.	as expected
AO-22 Tool calculates hashes by block.	option not available
AO-23 Logged information is correct.	as expected
AO-24 Source is unchanged by acquisition.	not checked

Analysis: Expected results not achieved

5.2.30   DA-10-E

Test Case DA-10-E AccessData FTK Imager CLI v2.9	
Case Summary:	DA-10 Acquire a digital source to an image file in an alternate format.
Assertions:	AM-01 The tool uses access interface SRC-AI to access the digital source. AM-02 The tool acquires digital source DS. AM-03 The tool executes in execution environment XE. AM-05 If image file creation is specified, the tool creates an image file on file system type FS. AM-06 All visible sectors are acquired from the digital source. AM-08 All sectors acquired from the digital source are acquired accurately. AO-01 If the tool creates an image file, the data represented by the image file is the same as the data acquired by the tool. AO-02 If an image file format is specified, the tool creates an image file in the specified format. AO-05 If the tool creates a multi-file image of a requested size then all the individual files shall be no larger than the requested size. AO-22 If requested, the tool calculates block hashes for a specified block size during an acquisition for each block acquired from the digital source. AO-23 If the tool logs any log significant information, the information is accurately recorded in the log file. AO-24 If the tool executes in a forensically safe execution environment, the digital source is unchanged by the acquisition process.
Tester Name:	csr
Test Host:	DeathStar
Test Date:	Mon Apr 9 07:25:06 2012
Drives:	src(01-IDE) dst (none) other (20-LAP)
Source Setup:	src hash (SHA1): < A48BB5665D6DC57C22DB68E2F723DA9AA8DF82B9 > src hash (MD5): < F458F673894753FA6A0EC8B8EC63848E > 78165360 total sectors (40020664320 bytes) Model (0BB-00JHC0) serial # (WD-WMAMC74171) N Start LBA Length Start C/H/S End C/H/S boot Partition type 1 P 000000063 020980827 0000/001/01 1023/254/63 0C Fat32X 2 X 020980890 057175335 1023/000/01 1023/254/63 0F extended 3 S 000000063 000032067 1023/001/01 1023/254/63 01 Fat12 4 x 000032130 002104515 1023/000/01 1023/254/63 05 extended 5 S 000000063 002104452 1023/001/01 1023/254/63 06 Fat16 6 x 002136645 004192965 1023/000/01 1023/254/63 05 extended 7 S 000000063 004192902 1023/001/01 1023/254/63 16 other 8 x 006329610 008401995 1023/000/01 1023/254/63 05 extended 9 S 000000063 008401932 1023/001/01 1023/254/63 0B Fat32 10 x 014731605 010490445 1023/000/01 1023/254/63 05 extended 11 S 000000063 010490382 1023/001/01 1023/254/63 83 Linux 12 x 025222050 004209030 1023/000/01 1023/254/63 05 extended 13 S 000000063 004208967 1023/001/01 1023/254/63 82 Linux swap 14 x 029431080 027744255 1023/000/01 1023/254/63 05 extended 15 S 000000063 027744192 1023/001/01 1023/254/63 07 NTFS 16 S 000000000 000000000 0000/000/00 0000/000/00 00 empty entry 17 P 000000000 000000000 0000/000/00 0000/000/00 00 empty entry 18 P 000000000 000000000 0000/000/00 0000/000/00 00 empty entry 1 020980827 sectors 10742183424 bytes 3 000032067 sectors 16418304 bytes 5 002104452 sectors 1077479424 bytes 7 004192902 sectors 2146765824 bytes 9 008401932 sectors 4301789184 bytes 11 010490382 sectors 5371075584 bytes 13 004208967 sectors 2154991104 bytes 15 027744192 sectors 14205026304 bytes
Log Highlights:	====== Tool Settings: ====== image format: Encrypted image size: 40020664832 MB Write Block: 3 Fastbloc IDE OS: Linux debian 2.6.32-5-486 #1 Mon Oct 3 03:34:28 UTC 2011 i686 GNU/Linux

```
====== Image file segments ======
    1 40020664832 2012-04-10 08:55 da-10-E.001
    2        1098 2012-04-10 09:12 da-10-E.001.txt
    3           0 2012-04-10 09:31 ls.txt
======== Excerpt from Tool log ========
Case: da-10-e
Drive Geometry:
 Cylinders: 4865
 Heads: 255
 Sectors per Track: 63
 Bytes per Sector: 512
 Sector Count: 78165360
Physical Drive Information:
 Drive Model: ATA WDC WD400BB-00JH
 Drive Interface Type: SCSI
 Source data size: 38166 MB
 Sector count:   78165360
Source hash:
 MD5:    f458f673894753fa6a0ec8b8ec63848e
 MD5:    a3d947d9ea072ed111986f62f20c352c : FAILED
 SHA1:   a48bb5665d6dc57c22db68e2f723da9aa8df82b9
 SHA1:   70d708a1999236188bd72ff7d49e538d70b3294b : FAILED
Verification hash:
Segment list:
 /media/xxx/da-10-E.001
======== End of Excerpt from Tool log ========
```

	Assertion & Expected Result	Actual Result
Results:	AM-01 Source acquired using interface AI.	as expected
	AM-02 Source is type DS.	as expected
	AM-03 Execution environment is XE.	as expected
	AM-05 An image is created on file system type FS.	as expected
	AM-06 All visible sectors acquired.	as expected
	AM-08 All sectors accurately acquired.	as expected
	AO-01 Image file is complete and accurate.	as expected
	AO-02 Image file in specified format.	as expected
	AO-05 Multifile image created.	as expected
	AO-22 Tool calculates hashes by block.	option not available
	AO-23 Logged information is correct.	as expected
	AO-24 Source is unchanged by acquisition.	not checked
Analysis:	Expected results achieved	

5.2.31　DA-10-E01

Test Case DA-10-E01 AccessData FTK Imager CLI v2.9	
Case Summary:	DA-10 Acquire a digital source to an image file in an alternate format.
Assertions:	AM-01 The tool uses access interface SRC-AI to access the digital source. AM-02 The tool acquires digital source DS. AM-03 The tool executes in execution environment XE. AM-05 If image file creation is specified, the tool creates an image file on file system type FS. AM-06 All visible sectors are acquired from the digital source. AM-08 All sectors acquired from the digital source are acquired accurately. AO-01 If the tool creates an image file, the data represented by the image file is the same as the data acquired by the tool. AO-02 If an image file format is specified, the tool creates an image file in the specified format. AO-05 If the tool creates a multi-file image of a requested size then all the individual files shall be no larger than the requested size. AO-22 If requested, the tool calculates block hashes for a specified block size during an acquisition for each block acquired from the digital source. AO-23 If the tool logs any log significant information, the information is accurately recorded in the log file. AO-24 If the tool executes in a forensically safe execution environment, the digital source is unchanged by the acquisition process.
Tester Name:	csr
Test Host:	DeathStar
Test Date:	Wed Apr 4 13:09:10 2012
Drives:	src(41) dst (none) other (29-LAP)
Source Setup:	src hash (SHA256): < FBF3AA21489653D880FFAE71449A9F7E8EE4F56A6C3BF58A3A3FFB13203F1B1D > src hash (SHA1): < 15CAA1A307271160D8372668BF8A03FC45A51CC9 > src hash (MD5): < 0A6A8EF78BDC14E2026710D8CCB5607C > 78125000 total sectors (40000000000 bytes) 65534/015/63 (max cyl/hd values) 65535/016/63 (number of cyl/hd) IDE disk: Model (WDC WD400BB-75JHC0) serial # (WD-WMAMC4658355) N Start LBA Length Start C/H/S End C/H/S boot Partition type 1 P 000000063 078107967 0000/001/01 1023/254/63 Boot 07 NTFS 2 P 000000000 000000000 0000/000/00 0000/000/00 00 empty entry 3 P 000000000 000000000 0000/000/00 0000/000/00 00 empty entry 4 P 000000000 000000000 0000/000/00 0000/000/00 00 empty entry 1 078107967 sectors 39991279104 bytes

Log Highlights:	====== Tool Settings: ======
	image format: e01
	imape size: 952647657 MB
	
	Write Block: 3 Fastbloc IDE
	
	OS: Linux debian 2.6.32-5-486 #1 Mon Oct 3 03:34:28 UTC 2011 i686 GNU/Linux
	
	====== Image file segments ======
	    1 952647657 2012-04-04 13:42 da-10.E01
	    2 1098 2012-04-04 13:45 logfile.txt
	    3 0 2012-04-04 13:46 ls.txt
	======== Excerpt from Tool log ========
	Case: da-10-e01
	Drive Geometry:
	 Cylinders: 4863
	 Heads: 255
	 Sectors per Track: 63
	 Bytes per Sector: 512
	 Sector Count: 78125000
	Physical Drive Information:
	 Drive Model: ATA WDC WD400BB-75JH

Test Case DA-10-E01 AccessData FTK Imager CLI v2.9	

	Drive Interface Type: SCSI
	Source data size: 38146 MB
	Sector count: 78125000
	Source hash:
	  MD5: 0a6a8ef78bdc14e2026710d8ccb5607c
	  SHA1: 15caa1a307271160d8372668bf8a03fc45a51cc9
	Verification hash:
	  MD5: 0a6a8ef78bdc14e2026710d8ccb5607c
	  SHA1: 15caa1a307271160d8372668bf8a03fc45a51cc9
	Segment list:
	  /media/xxx/da-10.E01
	======== End of Excerpt from Tool log ========

Results:	

Assertion & Expected Result	Actual Result
AM-01 Source acquired using interface AI.	as expected
AM-02 Source is type DS.	as expected
AM-03 Execution environment is XE.	as expected
AM-05 An image is created on file system type FS.	as expected
AM-06 All visible sectors acquired.	as expected
AM-08 All sectors accurately acquired.	as expected
AO-01 Image file is complete and accurate.	as expected
AO-02 Image file in specified format.	as expected
AO-05 Multifile image created.	as expected
AO-22 Tool calculates hashes by block.	option not available
AO-23 Logged information is correct.	as expected
AO-24 Source is unchanged by acquisition.	not checked

Analysis:	Expected results achieved

5.2.32   DA-10-S01

Test Case DA-10-S01 AccessData FTK Imager CLI v2.9	
Case Summary:	DA-10 Acquire a digital source to an image file in an alternate format.
Assertions:	AM-01 The tool uses access interface SRC-AI to access the digital source. AM-02 The tool acquires digital source DS. AM-03 The tool executes in execution environment XE. AM-05 If image file creation is specified, the tool creates an image file on file system type FS. AM-06 All visible sectors are acquired from the digital source. AM-08 All sectors acquired from the digital source are acquired accurately. AO-01 If the tool creates an image file, the data represented by the image file is the same as the data acquired by the tool. AO-02 If an image file format is specified, the tool creates an image file in the specified format. AO-05 If the tool creates a multi-file image of a requested size then all the individual files shall be no larger than the requested size. AO-22 If requested, the tool calculates block hashes for a specified block size during an acquisition for each block acquired from the digital source. AO-23 If the tool logs any log significant information, the information is accurately recorded in the log file. AO-24 If the tool executes in a forensically safe execution environment, the digital source is unchanged by the acquisition process.
Tester Name:	csr
Test Host:	DeathStar
Test Date:	Wed Apr 5 13:09:10 2012
Drives:	src(41) dst (none) other (29-LAP)
Source Setup:	src hash (SHA256): < FBF3AA21489653D880FFAE71449A9F7E8EE4F56A6C3BF58A3A3FFB13203F1B1D > src hash (SHA1): < 15CAA1A307271160D8372668BF8A03FC45A51CC9 > src hash (MD5): < 0A6A8EF78BDC14E2026710D8CCB5607C > 78125000 total sectors (40000000000 bytes) 65534/015/63 (max cyl/hd values) 65535/016/63 (number of cyl/hd) IDE disk: Model (WDC WD400BB-75JHC0) serial # (WD-WMAMC4658355) N Start LBA Length Start C/H/S End C/H/S boot Partition type 1 P 000000063 078107967 0000/001/01 1023/254/63 Boot 07 NTFS 2 P 000000000 000000000 0000/000/00 0000/000/00 00 empty entry 3 P 000000000 000000000 0000/000/00 0000/000/00 00 empty entry 4 P 000000000 000000000 0000/000/00 0000/000/00 00 empty entry 1 078107967 sectors 39991279104 bytes

Log Highlights:	====== Tool Settings: ======
	image format: s01
	image size: 947798214 MB
	
	Write Block: 3 Fastbloc IDE
	
	OS: Linux debian 2.6.32-5-486 #1 Mon Oct 3 03:34:28 UTC 2011 i686 GNU/Linux
	
	====== Image file segments ======
	    1 947798214 2012-04-05 13:01 da-10.s01
	    2 1098 2012-04-05 13:04 da-10.s01.txt
	======== Excerpt from Tool log ========
	Case: da-10-s01
	Drive Geometry:
	 Cylinders: 4863
	 Heads: 255
	 Sectors per Track: 63
	 Bytes per Sector: 512
	 Sector Count: 78125000
	Physical Drive Information:
	 Drive Model: ATA WDC WD400BB-75JH

```
            Drive Interface Type: SCSI
            Source data size: 38146 MB
            Sector count:    78125000
          Source hash:
           MD5:    0a6a8ef78bdc14e2026710d8ccb5607c
           SHA1:   15caa1a307271160d8372668bf8a03fc45a51cc9
          Verification hash:
           MD5:    0a6a8ef78bdc14e2026710d8ccb5607c
           SHA1:   15caa1a307271160d8372668bf8a03fc45a51cc9
          Segment list:
           /media/xxx/da-10.s01
          ======== End of Excerpt from Tool log ========
```

Results:	

Assertion & Expected Result	Actual Result
AM-01 Source acquired using interface AI.	as expected
AM-02 Source is type DS.	as expected
AM-03 Execution environment is XE.	as expected
AM-05 An image is created on file system type FS.	as expected
AM-06 All visible sectors acquired.	as expected
AM-08 All sectors accurately acquired.	as expected
AO-01 Image file is complete and accurate.	as expected
AO-02 Image file in specified format.	as expected
AO-05 Multifile image created.	as expected
AO-22 Tool calculates hashes by block.	option not available
AO-23 Logged information is correct.	as expected
AO-24 Source is unchanged by acquisition.	not checked

Analysis:	Expected results achieved

5.2.33   DA-12

Test Case DA-12 AccessData FTK Imager CLI v2.9	
Case Summary:	DA-12 Attempt to create an image file where there is insufficient space.
Assertions:	AM-01 The tool uses access interface SRC-AI to access the digital source. AM-02 The tool acquires digital source DS. AM-03 The tool executes in execution environment XE. AM-05 If image file creation is specified, the tool creates an image file on file system type FS. AO-04 If the tool is creating an image file and there is insufficient space on the image destination device to contain the image file, the tool shall notify the user. AO-23 If the tool logs any log significant information, the information is accurately recorded in the log file. AO-24 If the tool executes in a forensically safe execution environment, the digital source is unchanged by the acquisition process.
Tester Name:	csr
Test Host:	DeathStar
Test Date:	Mon Mar 19 07:31:13 2012
Drives:	src(4F) dst (none) other (5D-SATA)
Source Setup:	src hash (SHA1): < 51FE53FD6BF7B7B69A875EDBD9AC01D41194C78C > src hash (MD5): < A98DF276339451CE9E701D087E2BFC95 > 488397168 total sectors (250059350016 bytes) 30400/254/63 (max cyl/hd values) 30401/255/63 (number of cyl/hd) IDE disk: Model (WDC WD2500JB-00EVA0) serial # (WD-WMAEH2681554) N Start LBA Length Start C/H/S End C/H/S boot Partition type 1 P 000000063 268413957 0000/001/01 1023/254/63 Boot 07 NTFS 2 P 000000000 000000000 0000/000/00 0000/000/00 00 empty entry 3 P 000000000 000000000 0000/000/00 0000/000/00 00 empty entry 4 P 000000000 000000000 0000/000/00 0000/000/00 00 empty entry 1 268413957 sectors 137427945984 bytes

Log Highlights:	====== Tool Message: ======
	root@ubuntu:/media/xxx# ftkimager /dev/sdb /media/xxx/da-12 --e01 --verify
	AccessData FTK Imager v2.9 CLI (May 12 2010)
	Copyright 2006-2010 AccessData Corp., 384 South 400 West, Lindon, UT 84042
	All rights reserved.
	
	Creating image...
	105011.09 / 238475.19 MB (53.96 MB/sec) - 0:41:13 left
	Image creation failed: No space left on device (28)
	
	====== Tool Settings: ======
	image:238475 MB
	image format: e01
	
	OS: Linux debian 2.6.32-5-486 #1 Mon Oct 3 03:34:28 UTC 2011 i686 GNU/Linux
	
	====== Image file segments ======
	    1 2107817984 2012-03-19 14:22 da-12.E01
	    2 16384 2012-03-19 13:48 lost+found
	    3 0 2012-03-19 14:38 ls.txt

Results:	

Assertion & Expected Result	Actual Result
AM-01 Source acquired using interface AI.	as expected
AM-02 Source is type DS.	as expected
AM-03 Execution environment is XE.	as expected
AM-05 An image is created on file system type FS.	as expected
AO-04 User notified if space exhausted.	as expected
AO-23 Logged information is correct.	as expected
AO-24 Source is unchanged by acquisition.	not checked

Analysis:	Expected results achieved

5.2.34   DA-14-ATA28

Test Case DA-14-ATA28 AccessData FTK Imager CLI v2.9	
Case Summary:	DA-14 Create an unaligned clone from an image file.
Assertions:	AM-03 The tool executes in execution environment XE. AO-12 If requested, a clone is created from an image file. AO-13 A clone is created using access interface DST-AI to write to the clone device. AO-14 If an unaligned clone is created, each sector written to the clone is accurately written to the same disk address on the clone that the sector occupied on the digital source. AO-17 If requested, any excess sectors on a clone destination device are not modified. AO-23 If the tool logs any log significant information, the information is accurately recorded in the log file.
Tester Name:	csr
Test Host:	DeathStar
Test Date:	Thu Aug 23 12:46:31 2012
Drives:	src(41) dst (24-LAP) other (0F-FU)
Source Setup:	src hash (SHA256): < FBF3AA21489653D880FFAE71449A9F7E8EE4F56A6C3BF58A3A3FFB13203F1B1D > src hash (SHA1): < 15CAA1A307271160D8372668BF8A03FC45A51CC9 > src hash (MD5): < 0A6A8EF78BDC14E2026710D8CCB5607C > 78125000 total sectors (40000000000 bytes) 65534/015/63 (max cyl/hd values) 65535/016/63 (number of cyl/hd) IDE disk: Model (WDC WD400BB-75JHC0) serial # (WD-WMAMC4658355) N Start LBA Length Start C/H/S End C/H/S boot Partition type 1 P 000000063 078107967 0000/001/01 1023/254/63 Boot 07 NTFS 2 P 000000000 000000000 0000/000/00 0000/000/00 00 empty entry 3 P 000000000 000000000 0000/000/00 0000/000/00 00 empty entry 4 P 000000000 000000000 0000/000/00 0000/000/00 00 empty entry 1 078107967 sectors 39991279104 bytes
Log Highlights:	====== Destination drive setup ====== 78140160 sectors wiped with 24 ====== Comparison of original to clone drive ====== Sectors compared: 78125000 Sectors match: 78125000 Sectors differ: 0 Bytes differ: 0 Diffs range Source (78125000) has 15160 fewer sectors than destination (78140160) Zero fill: 0 Src Byte fill (41): 0 Dst Byte fill (24): 15160 Other fill: 0 Other no fill: 0 Zero fill range: Src fill range: Dst fill range: 78125000-78140159 Other fill range: Other not filled range: 0 source read errors, 0 destination read errors OS: Linux debian 2.6.32-5-486 #1 Mon Oct 3 03:34:28 UTC 2011 i686 GNU/Linux
Results:	

Assertion & Expected Result	Actual Result
AM-03 Execution environment is XE.	as expected
AO-12 A clone is created from an image file.	as expected
AO-13 Clone created using interface AI.	as expected
AO-14 An unaligned clone is created.	as expected
AO-17 Excess sectors are unchanged.	as expected

	AO-23 Logged information is correct.	as expected
Analysis:	Expected results achieved	

5.2.35   DA-14-ATA48

Test Case DA-14-ATA48 AccessData FTK Imager CLI v2.9	
Case Summary:	DA-14 Create an unaligned clone from an image file.
Assertions:	AM-03 The tool executes in execution environment XE. AO-12 If requested, a clone is created from an image file. AO-13 A clone is created using access interface DST-AI to write to the clone device. AO-14 If an unaligned clone is created, each sector written to the clone is accurately written to the same disk address on the clone that the sector occupied on the digital source. AO-17 If requested, any excess sectors on a clone destination device are not modified. AO-23 If the tool logs any log significant information, the information is accurately recorded in the log file.
Tester Name:	csr
Test Host:	DeathStar
Test Date:	Wed Mar 7 16:26:09 2012
Drives:	src(4F) dst (2A-IDE) other (none)
Source Setup:	src hash (SHA1): < 51FE53FD6BF7B7B69A875EDBD9AC01D41194C78C > src hash (MD5): < A98DF276339451CE9E701D087E2BFC95 > 488397168 total sectors (250059350016 bytes) 30400/254/63 (max cyl/hd values) 30401/255/63 (number of cyl/hd) IDE disk: Model (WDC WD2500JB-00EVA0) serial # (WD-WMAEH2681554) N Start LBA Length Start C/H/S End C/H/S boot Partition type 1 P 000000063 268413957 0000/001/01 1023/254/63 Boot 07 NTFS 2 P 000000000 000000000 0000/000/00 0000/000/00 00 empty entry 3 P 000000000 000000000 0000/000/00 0000/000/00 00 empty entry 4 P 000000000 000000000 0000/000/00 0000/000/00 00 empty entry 1 268413957 sectors 137427945984 bytes
Log Highlights:	====== Destination drive setup ====== 490234752 sectors wiped with 2A ====== Comparison of original to clone drive ====== Sectors compared: 488397168 Sectors match: 488397168 Sectors differ: 0 Bytes differ: 0 Diffs range Source (488397168) has 1837584 fewer sectors than destination (490234752) Zero fill: 0 Src Byte fill (4F): 0 Dst Byte fill (2A): 1837584 Other fill: 0 Other no fill: 0 Zero fill range: Src fill range: Dst fill range: 488397168-490234751 Other fill range: Other not filled range: 0 source read errors, 0 destination read errors Write Block: 3 FASTBloc IDE OS: Linux ubuntu 2.6.32-33-generic #70-Ubuntu SMP Thu Jul 7 21:09:46 UTC 2011 i686 GNU/Linux
Results:	

Assertion & Expected Result	Actual Result
AM-03 Execution environment is XE.	as expected
AO-12 A clone is created from an image file.	as expected
AO-13 Clone created using interface AI.	as expected
AO-14 An unaligned clone is created.	as expected
AO-17 Excess sectors are unchanged.	as expected

Test Case DA-14-ATA48 AccessData FTK Imager CLI v2.9		
	AO-23 Logged information is correct.	as expected
Analysis:	Expected results achieved	

5.2.36   DA-14-CF

Test Case DA-14-CF AccessData FTK Imager CLI v2.9	
Case Summary:	DA-14 Create an unaligned clone from an image file.
Assertions:	AM-03 The tool executes in execution environment XE. AO-12 If requested, a clone is created from an image file. AO-13 A clone is created using access interface DST-AI to write to the clone device. AO-14 If an unaligned clone is created, each sector written to the clone is accurately written to the same disk address on the clone that the sector occupied on the digital source. AO-17 If requested, any excess sectors on a clone destination device are not modified. AO-23 If the tool logs any log significant information, the information is accurately recorded in the log file.
Tester Name:	csr
Test Host:	DeathStar
Test Date:	Mon Mar 26 09:39:25 2012
Drives:	src(C1-CF) dst (C2-CF) other (none)
Source Setup:	src hash (SHA256): < C7CF0218222DF80D5316511D6814266C7FA507C13F795AD3D323BB73C1590D80 > src hash (SHA1): < 5B8235178DF99FA307430C088F81746606638A0B > src hash (MD5): < 776DF8B4D2589E21DEBCF589EDC16D78 > 503808 total sectors (257949696 bytes) Model (CF) serial # () N Start LBA Length Start C/H/S End C/H/S boot Partition type 1 P 778135908 1141509631 0357/116/40 0357/032/45 Boot 72 other 2 P 168689522 1936028240 0288/115/43 0367/114/50 Boot 65 other 3 P 1869881465 1936028192 0366/032/33 0357/032/43 Boot 79 other 4 P 2885681152 000055499 0372/097/50 0000/010/00 Boot 0D other 1 1141509631 sectors 584452931072 bytes 2 1936028240 sectors 991246458880 bytes 3 1936028192 sectors 991246434304 bytes 4 000055499 sectors 28415488 bytes
Log Highlights:	====== Destination drive setup ====== 503808 sectors wiped with C2 ====== Comparison of original to clone drive ====== Sectors compared: 503808 Sectors match: 503808 Sectors differ: 0 Bytes differ: 0 Diffs range 0 source read errors, 0 destination read errors Write Block: 7 UltraBlock Forensic Card Reader OS: Linux debian 2.6.32-5-486 #1 Mon Oct 3 03:34:28 UTC 2011 i686 GNU/Linux
Results:	<table><tr><th>Assertion & Expected Result</th><th>Actual Result</th></tr><tr><td>AM-03 Execution environment is XE.</td><td>as expected</td></tr><tr><td>AO-12 A clone is created from an image file.</td><td>as expected</td></tr><tr><td>AO-13 Clone created using interface AI.</td><td>as expected</td></tr><tr><td>AO-14 An unaligned clone is created.</td><td>as expected</td></tr><tr><td>AO-17 Excess sectors are unchanged.</td><td>as expected</td></tr><tr><td>AO-23 Logged information is correct.</td><td>as expected</td></tr></table>
Analysis:	Expected results achieved

5.2.37 DA-14-E

Test Case DA-14-E AccessData FTK Imager CLI v2.9	
Case Summary:	DA-14 Create an unaligned clone from an image file.
Assertions:	AM-03 The tool executes in execution environment XE. AO-12 If requested, a clone is created from an image file. AO-13 A clone is created using access interface DST-AI to write to the clone device. AO-14 If an unaligned clone is created, each sector written to the clone is accurately written to the same disk address on the clone that the sector occupied on the digital source. AO-17 If requested, any excess sectors on a clone destination device are not modified. AO-23 If the tool logs any log significant information, the information is accurately recorded in the log file.
Tester Name:	csr
Test Host:	DeathStar
Test Date:	Mon May 25 09:39:25 2012
Drives:	src (01-IDE) dst (6F) other (none)

Source Setup:	src hash (SHA1): < A48BB5665D6DC57C22DB68E2F723DA9AA8DF82B9 >
	src hash (MD5): < F458F673894753FA6A0EC8B8EC63848E >
	78165360 total sectors (40020664320 bytes)
	Model (0BB-00JHC0) serial # (WD-WMAMC74171)
	<pre> N Start LBA Length Start C/H/S End C/H/S boot Partition type
	  1 P 000000063 020980827 0000/001/01 1023/254/63 0C Fat32X
	  2 X 020980890 057175335 1023/000/01 1023/254/63 0F extended
	  3 S 000000063 000032067 1023/001/01 1023/254/63 01 Fat12
	  4 x 000032130 002104515 1023/000/01 1023/254/63 05 extended
	  5 S 000000063 002104452 1023/001/01 1023/254/63 06 Fat16
	  6 x 002136645 004192965 1023/000/01 1023/254/63 05 extended
	  7 S 000000063 004192902 1023/001/01 1023/254/63 16 other
	  8 x 006329610 008401995 1023/000/01 1023/254/63 05 extended
	  9 S 000000063 008401932 1023/001/01 1023/254/63 0B Fat32
	 10 x 014731605 010490445 1023/000/01 1023/254/63 05 extended
	 11 S 000000063 010490382 1023/001/01 1023/254/63 83 Linux
	 12 x 025222050 004209030 1023/000/01 1023/254/63 05 extended
	 13 S 000000063 004208967 1023/001/01 1023/254/63 82 Linux swap
	 14 x 029431080 027744255 1023/000/01 1023/254/63 05 extended
	 15 S 000000063 027744192 1023/001/01 1023/254/63 07 NTFS
	 16 S 000000000 000000000 0000/000/00 0000/000/00 00 empty entry
	 17 P 000000000 000000000 0000/000/00 0000/000/00 00 empty entry
	 18 P 000000000 000000000 0000/000/00 0000/000/00 00 empty entry
	 1 020980827 sectors 10742183424 bytes
	 3 000032067 sectors 16418304 bytes
	 5 002104452 sectors 1077479424 bytes
	 7 004192902 sectors 2146765824 bytes
	 9 008401932 sectors 4301789184 bytes
	11 010490382 sectors 5371075584 bytes
	13 004208967 sectors 2154991104 bytes
	15 027744192 sectors 14205026304 bytes</pre>

Log Highlights:	====== Destination drive setup ====== 120103200 sectors wiped with 6F ====== Comparison of original to clone drive ====== Sectors compared: 78165360 Sectors match: 78165360 Sectors differ: 0 Bytes differ: 0 Diffs range Source (78165360) has 41937840 fewer sectors than destination (120103200) Zero fill: 0 Src Byte fill (01): 0 Dst Byte fill (6F): 41937840 Other fill: 0 Other no fill: 0 Zero fill range:

```
Src fill range:
Dst fill range:  78165360-120103199
Other fill range:
Other not filled range:
0 source read errors, 0 destination read errors


====== Tool Settings: ======
fill: none

Write Block: 3 FASTBloc IDE

OS: Linux ubuntu 2.6.32-33-generic #70-Ubuntu SMP Thu Jul 7 21:09:46 UTC
2011 i686 GNU/Linux

======== Excerpt from Tool log ========
Case: da-14-e
Drive Geometry:
 Bytes per Sector: 512
 Sector Count: 78165360
Physical Drive Information:
 Source data size: 38166 MB
 Sector count:    78165360
Source hash:
 MD5:    f458f673894753fa6a0ec8b8ec63848e
 SHA1:   a48bb5665d6dc57c22db68e2f723da9aa8df82b9
Verification hash:
 MD5:    f458f673894753fa6a0ec8b8ec63848e
 SHA1:   a48bb5665d6dc57c22db68e2f723da9aa8df82b9
Segment list:
  /media/xxx/da-14-E.001
======== End of Excerpt from Tool log ========
```

Results:

Assertion & Expected Result	Actual Result
AM-03 Execution environment is XE.	as expected
AO-12 A clone is created from an image file.	as expected
AO-13 Clone created using interface AI.	as expected
AO-14 An unaligned clone is created.	as expected
AO-17 Excess sectors are unchanged.	as expected
AO-23 Logged information is correct.	as expected

Analysis: | Expected results achieved

5.2.38　DA-14-E01

Test Case DA-14-E01 AccessData FTK Imager CLI v2.9	
Case Summary:	DA-14 Create an unaligned clone from an image file.
Assertions:	AM-03 The tool executes in execution environment XE. AO-12 If requested, a clone is created from an image file. AO-13 A clone is created using access interface DST-AI to write to the clone device. AO-14 If an unaligned clone is created, each sector written to the clone is accurately written to the same disk address on the clone that the sector occupied on the digital source. AO-17 If requested, any excess sectors on a clone destination device are not modified. AO-23 If the tool logs any log significant information, the information is accurately recorded in the log file.
Tester Name:	csr
Test Host:	DeathStar
Test Date:	Wed Apr 4 13:48:38 2012
Drives:	src(41) dst (6f) other (none)

Source Setup:	src hash (SHA256): <
	 FBF3AA21489653D880FFAE71449A9F7E8EE4F56A6C3BF58A3A3FFB13203F1B1D >
	 src hash (SHA1): < 15CAA1A307271160D8372668BF8A03FC45A51CC9 >
	 src hash (MD5): < 0A6A8EF78BDC14E2026710D8CCB5607C >
	 78125000 total sectors (40000000000 bytes)
	 65534/015/63 (max cyl/hd values)
	 65535/016/63 (number of cyl/hd)
	 IDE disk: Model (WDC WD400BB-75JHC0) serial # (WD-WMAMC4658355)
	  N Start LBA Length Start C/H/S End C/H/S boot Partition type
	  1 P 000000063 078107967 0000/001/01 1023/254/63 Boot 07 NTFS
	  2 P 000000000 000000000 0000/000/00 0000/000/00 00 empty entry
	  3 P 000000000 000000000 0000/000/00 0000/000/00 00 empty entry
	  4 P 000000000 000000000 0000/000/00 0000/000/00 00 empty entry
	 1 078107967 sectors 39991279104 bytes

Log Highlights:	====== Destination drive setup ====== 120103200 sectors wiped with 6F ====== Comparison of original to clone drive ====== Sectors compared: 78125000 Sectors match: 78125000 Sectors differ: 0 Bytes differ: 0 Diffs range Source (78125000) has 41978200 fewer sectors than destination (120103200) Zero fill: 0 Src Byte fill (41): 0 Dst Byte fill (6F): 41978200 Other fill: 0 Other no fill: 0 Zero fill range: Src fill range: Dst fill range: 78125000-120103199 Other fill range: Other not filled range: 0 source read errors, 0 destination read errors ====== Tool Settings: ====== fill: none OS: Linux
Results:	

Assertion & Expected Result	Actual Result
AM-03 Execution environment is XE.	as expected

Test Case DA-14-E01 AccessData FTK Imager CLI v2.9		
	AO-12 A clone is created from an image file.	as expected
	AO-13 Clone created using interface AI.	as expected
	AO-14 An unaligned clone is created.	as expected
	AO-17 Excess sectors are unchanged.	as expected
	AO-23 Logged information is correct.	as expected
Analysis:	Expected results achieved	

5.2.39   DA-14-EXT3

Test Case DA-14-EXT3 AccessData FTK Imager CLI v2.9	
Case Summary:	DA-14 Create an unaligned clone from an image file.
Assertions:	AM-03 The tool executes in execution environment XE. AO-12 If requested, a clone is created from an image file. AO-13 A clone is created using access interface DST-AI to write to the clone device. AO-14 If an unaligned clone is created, each sector written to the clone is accurately written to the same disk address on the clone that the sector occupied on the digital source. AO-17 If requested, any excess sectors on a clone destination device are not modified. AO-23 If the tool logs any log significant information, the information is accurately recorded in the log file.
Tester Name:	csr
Test Host:	DeathStar
Test Date:	Wed Apr 18 08:34:13 2012
Drives:	src (49-SATA) dst (31-IDE) other (none)

Source Setup:	src hash (SHA1): < 6EC98F42EB5914D1F9D1661C0BB0A3660569F95B >
	src hash (MD5): < 30BAB74F67783C0555BCBD73DD4D0D5E >
	156301488 total sectors (80026361856 bytes)
	Model (ST380815AS) serial # (5QZ5TD8Y)
	  N Start LBA Length Start C/H/S End C/H/S boot Partition type
	  1 P 000002048 010485760 0000/032/33 0652/213/09 07 NTFS
	  2 P 010490445 005863725 0653/000/01 1017/254/63 83 Linux
	  3 P 016354170 007807590 1018/000/01 1023/254/63 83 Linux
	  4 P 000000000 000000000 0000/000/00 0000/000/00 00 empty entry
	1 010485760 sectors 5368709120 bytes
	2 005863725 sectors 3002227200 bytes
	3 007807590 sectors 3997486080 bytes
	49-SATAEXT3-md5sum 5863725 A25176AE775F65181DAC8C8D051DDF5D
	49-SATAEXT3-sha1sum 5863725 FDF0F2BA2D4CB2D45E45717213AE218880236418
	Excess destination partition sectors hash:
	SHA1 3002227200 - 3224277503 = 59713F6560C148A1A8FC6AC00FE6D48CDDB7CB74

Log Highlights:	====== Destination drive setup ====== 35673120 sectors wiped with 31 ====== Comparison of original to clone drive ====== Sectors compared: 5863725 Sectors match: 5863725 Sectors differ: 0 Bytes differ: 0 Diffs range: Source (5863725) has 433692 fewer sectors than destination (6297417) Zero fill: 8081 Src Byte fill (49): 0 Dst Byte fill (31): 425588 Other fill: 19 Other no fill: 4 Zero fill range: 6029313-6029320, 6029328-6033263, 6291464, 6291472-6295407, 6297216-6297415 Src fill range: Dst fill range: 5863725-6029311, 6033264-6291455, 6295408-6297215, 6297416 Other fill range: 6029322-6029327, 6291457-6291463, 6291466-6291471 Other not filled range: 6029312, 6029321, 6291456, 6291465 run start Wed Apr 18 09:31:38 2012 run finish Wed Apr 18 09:35:10 2012 elapsed time 0:3:32 Normal exit ====== Tool Settings: ====== fill: none

	Write Block: 11 TABLEAU SATA Bridge OS: Linux debian 2.6.32-5-486 #1 Mon Oct 3 03:34:28 UTC 2011 i686 GNU/Linux Excess destination partition sectors hash: SHA1 3002227200 - 3224277503 = 59713F6560C148A1A8FC6AC00FE6D48CDDB7CB74
Results:	

Assertion & Expected Result	Actual Result
AM-03 Execution environment is XE.	as expected
AO-12 A clone is created from an image file.	as expected
AO-13 Clone created using interface AI.	as expected
AO-14 An unaligned clone is created.	as expected
AO-17 Excess sectors are unchanged.	as expected
AO-23 Logged information is correct.	as expected

Analysis:	Expected results achieved

5.2.40   DA-14-EXT4

Test Case DA-14-EXT4 AccessData FTK Imager CLI v2.9	
Case Summary:	DA-14 Create an unaligned clone from an image file.
Assertions:	AM-03 The tool executes in execution environment XE. AO-12 If requested, a clone is created from an image file. AO-13 A clone is created using access interface DST-AI to write to the clone device. AO-14 If an unaligned clone is created, each sector written to the clone is accurately written to the same disk address on the clone that the sector occupied on the digital source. AO-17 If requested, any excess sectors on a clone destination device are not modified. AO-23 If the tool logs any log significant information, the information is accurately recorded in the log file.
Tester Name:	csr
Test Host:	DeathStar
Test Date:	Wed Apr 18 08:34:13 2012
Drives:	src(49-SATA) dst (31-IDE) other (none)
Source Setup:	src hash (SHA1): < 6EC98F42EB5914D1F9D1661C0BB0A3660569F95B > src hash (MD5): < 30BAB74F67783C0555BCBD73DD4D0D5E > 156301488 total sectors (80026361856 bytes) Model (ST380815AS) serial # (5QZ5TD8Y) N Start LBA Length Start C/H/S End C/H/S boot Partition type 1 P 000002048 010485760 0000/032/33 0652/213/09 07 NTFS 2 P 010490445 005863725 0653/000/01 1017/254/63 83 Linux 3 P 016354170 007807590 1018/000/01 1023/254/63 83 Linux 4 P 000000000 000000000 0000/000/00 0000/000/00 00 empty entry 1 010485760 sectors 5368709120 bytes 2 005863725 sectors 3002227200 bytes 3 007807590 sectors 3997486080 bytes 49-SATAEXT4-md5sum 7807590 567F2826AB468D69F97CB0D1878BE25D 49-SATAEXT4-sha1sum 7807590 F28A79F5E5CD28F859A1AC6B18A2CA3682D15A2A Excess destination partition sectors hash: SHA1 3997486080 - 4301789183 = 6E6D99EDC9E4D68300C2E0249EB6073C62F45B2B
Log Highlights:	====== Destination drive setup ====== 35673120 sectors wiped with 31 ====== Comparison of original to clone drive ====== Sectors compared: 7807590 Sectors match: 7807590 Sectors differ: 0 Bytes differ: 0 Diffs range: Source (7807590) has 594342 fewer sectors than destination (8401932) Zero fill: 136 Src Byte fill (49): 0 Dst Byte fill (31): 594198 Other fill: 7 Other no fill: 1 Zero fill range: 8401792-8401927 Src fill range: Dst fill range: 7807590-8388607, 8388616-8401791, 8401928-8401931 Other fill range: 8388609-8388615 Other not filled range: 8388608 run start Wed Apr 18 09:37:38 2012 run finish Wed Apr 18 09:42:51 2012 elapsed time 0:5:13 Normal exit ====== Tool Settings: ====== fill: none Write Block: 11 TABLEAU SATA Bridge

Test Case DA-14-EXT4 AccessData FTK Imager CLI v2.9	
	OS: Linux debian 2.6.32-5-486 #1 Mon Oct 3 03:34:28 UTC 2011 i686 GNU/Linux Excess destination partition sectors hash: SHA1 3997486080 - 4301789183 = 6E6D99EDC9E4D68300C2E0249EB6073C62F45B2B
Results:	

Assertion & Expected Result	Actual Result
AM-03 Execution environment is XE.	as expected
AO-12 A clone is created from an image file.	as expected
AO-13 Clone created using interface AI.	as expected
AO-14 An unaligned clone is created.	as expected
AO-17 Excess sectors are unchanged.	as expected
AO-23 Logged information is correct.	as expected

Analysis:	Expected results achieved

5.2.41   DA-14-F16

Test Case DA-14-F16 AccessData FTK Imager CLI v2.9	
Case Summary:	DA-14 Create an unaligned clone from an image file.
Assertions:	AM-03 The tool executes in execution environment XE. AO-12 If requested, a clone is created from an image file. AO-13 A clone is created using access interface DST-AI to write to the clone device. AO-14 If an unaligned clone is created, each sector written to the clone is accurately written to the same disk address on the clone that the sector occupied on the digital source. AO-17 If requested, any excess sectors on a clone destination device are not modified. AO-23 If the tool logs any log significant information, the information is accurately recorded in the log file.
Tester Name:	csr
Test Host:	DeathStar
Test Date:	Thu Mar 22 15:25:08 2012
Drives:	src(01-IDE) dst (08-IDE) other (none)

Source Setup:	src hash (SHA1): < A48BB5665D6DC57C22DB68E2F723DA9AA8DF82B9 >
	src hash (MD5): < F458F673894753FA6A0EC8B8EC63848E >
	78165360 total sectors (40020664320 bytes)
	Model (0BB-00JHC0) serial # (WD-WMAMC74171)
	<pre>N Start LBA Length Start C/H/S End C/H/S boot Partition type
	 1 P 000000063 020980827 0000/001/01 1023/254/63 0C Fat32X
	 2 X 020980890 057175335 1023/000/01 1023/254/63 0F extended
	 3 S 000000063 000032067 1023/001/01 1023/254/63 01 Fat12
	 4 x 000032130 002104515 1023/000/01 1023/254/63 05 extended
	 5 S 000000063 002104452 1023/001/01 1023/254/63 06 Fat16
	 6 x 002136645 004192965 1023/000/01 1023/254/63 05 extended
	 7 S 000000063 004192902 1023/001/01 1023/254/63 16 other
	 8 x 006329610 008401995 1023/000/01 1023/254/63 05 extended
	 9 S 000000063 008401932 1023/001/01 1023/254/63 0B Fat32
	10 x 014731605 010490445 1023/000/01 1023/254/63 05 extended
	11 S 000000063 010490382 1023/001/01 1023/254/63 83 Linux
	12 x 025222050 004209030 1023/000/01 1023/254/63 05 extended
	13 S 000000063 004208967 1023/001/01 1023/254/63 82 Linux swap
	14 x 029431080 027744255 1023/000/01 1023/254/63 05 extended
	15 S 000000063 027744192 1023/001/01 1023/254/63 07 NTFS
	16 S 000000000 000000000 0000/000/00 0000/000/00 00 empty entry
	17 P 000000000 000000000 0000/000/00 0000/000/00 00 empty entry
	18 P 000000000 000000000 0000/000/00 0000/000/00 00 empty entry
	 1 020980827 sectors 10742183424 bytes
	 3 000032067 sectors 16418304 bytes
	 5 002104452 sectors 1077479424 bytes
	 7 004192902 sectors 2146765824 bytes
	 9 008401932 sectors 4301789184 bytes
	11 010490382 sectors 5371075584 bytes
	13 004208967 sectors 2154991104 bytes
	15 027744192 sectors 14205026304 bytes</pre>01F16-md5 1077479423 8B24F3D793188AF2473F69B267AFDA42
	01F16-sha1 1077479423 074BA831B10132F4BF9F86AFAB37CB7FEF482C7D

Log Highlights:	====== Destination drive setup ====== 78165360 sectors wiped with 8 ====== Comparison of original to clone drive ====== Sectors compared: 2104452 Sectors match: 2104452 Sectors differ: 0 Bytes differ: 0 Diffs range: run start Fri Mar 23 12:24:18 2012 run finish Fri Mar 23 12:25:56 2012 elapsed time 0:1:38 Normal exit

```
====== Tool Settings: ======
fill: none

OS: Linux debian 2.6.32-5-486 #1 Mon Oct 3 03:34:28 UTC 2011 i686 GNU/Linux
```

Results:

Assertion & Expected Result	Actual Result
AM-03 Execution environment is XE.	as expected
AO-12 A clone is created from an image file.	as expected
AO-13 Clone created using interface AI.	as expected
AO-14 An unaligned clone is created.	as expected
AO-17 Excess sectors are unchanged.	as expected
AO-23 Logged information is correct.	as expected

Analysis: Expected results achieved

5.2.42   DA-14-F32

Test Case DA-14-F32 AccessData FTK Imager CLI v2.9	
Case Summary:	DA-14 Create an unaligned clone from an image file.
Assertions:	AM-03 The tool executes in execution environment XE. AO-12 If requested, a clone is created from an image file. AO-13 A clone is created using access interface DST-AI to write to the clone device. AO-14 If an unaligned clone is created, each sector written to the clone is accurately written to the same disk address on the clone that the sector occupied on the digital source. AO-17 If requested, any excess sectors on a clone destination device are not modified. AO-23 If the tool logs any log significant information, the information is accurately recorded in the log file.
Tester Name:	csr
Test Host:	DeathStar
Test Date:	Thu Mar 22 15:25:08 2012
Drives:	src(01-IDE) dst (08-IDE) other (none)

Source Setup:	src hash (SHA1): < A48BB5665D6DC57C22DB68E2F723DA9AA8DF82B9 >
	src hash (MD5): < F458F673894753FA6A0EC8B8EC63848E >
	78165360 total sectors (40020664320 bytes)
	Model (0BB-00JHC0) serial # (WD-WMAMC74171)
	<pre>N Start LBA Length Start C/H/S End C/H/S boot Partition type
	 1 P 000000063 020980827 0000/001/01 1023/254/63 0C Fat32X
	 2 X 020980890 057175335 1023/000/01 1023/254/63 0F extended
	 3 S 000000063 000032067 1023/001/01 1023/254/63 01 Fat12
	 4 x 000032130 002104515 1023/000/01 1023/254/63 05 extended
	 5 S 000000063 002104452 1023/001/01 1023/254/63 06 Fat16
	 6 x 002136645 004192965 1023/000/01 1023/254/63 05 extended
	 7 S 000000063 004192902 1023/001/01 1023/254/63 16 other
	 8 x 006329610 008401995 1023/000/01 1023/254/63 05 extended
	 9 S 000000063 008401932 1023/001/01 1023/254/63 0B Fat32
	10 x 014731605 010490445 1023/000/01 1023/254/63 05 extended
	11 S 000000063 010490382 1023/001/01 1023/254/63 83 Linux
	12 x 025222050 004209030 1023/000/01 1023/254/63 05 extended
	13 S 000000063 004208967 1023/001/01 1023/254/63 82 Linux swap
	14 x 029431080 027744255 1023/000/01 1023/254/63 05 extended
	15 S 000000063 027744192 1023/001/01 1023/254/63 07 NTFS
	16 S 000000000 000000000 0000/000/00 0000/000/00 00 empty entry
	17 P 000000000 000000000 0000/000/00 0000/000/00 00 empty entry
	18 P 000000000 000000000 0000/000/00 0000/000/00 00 empty entry</pre>
	1 020980827 sectors 10742183424 bytes
	3 000032067 sectors 16418304 bytes
	5 002104452 sectors 1077479424 bytes
	7 004192902 sectors 2146765824 bytes
	9 008401932 sectors 4301789184 bytes
	11 010490382 sectors 5371075584 bytes
	13 004208967 sectors 2154991104 bytes
	15 027744192 sectors 14205026304 bytes
	01F32-md5 4301789183 BFF7DC64C54339DA2A9D7972C076B514
	01F32-sha1 4301789183 B861D9E999F39750B484FFB693FF69DEC090C6B8
	01F32-sha256 4301789183
	CAE3A4CC33D59548063255D2AA4016940AC712DD96985AD9B94FF271CC3E943E

Log Highlights:	====== Destination drive setup ====== 78165360 sectors wiped with 8 ====== Comparison of original to clone drive ====== Sectors compared: 8401932 Sectors match: 8401932 Sectors differ: 0 Bytes differ: 0 Diffs range: run start Thu Mar 22 15:29:24 2012 run finish Thu Mar 22 15:32:44 2012

```
elapsed time 0:3:20
Normal exit


====== Tool Settings: ======
fill: none

OS: Linux debian 2.6.32-5-486 #1 Mon Oct 3 03:34:28 UTC 2011 i686 GNU/Linux
```

Results:

Assertion & Expected Result	Actual Result
AM-03 Execution environment is XE.	as expected
AO-12 A clone is created from an image file.	as expected
AO-13 Clone created using interface AI.	as expected
AO-14 An unaligned clone is created.	as expected
AO-17 Excess sectors are unchanged.	as expected
AO-23 Logged information is correct.	as expected

Analysis: Expected results achieved

5.2.43   DA-14-FW

Test Case DA-14-FW AccessData FTK Imager CLI v2.9	
Case Summary:	DA-14 Create an unaligned clone from an image file.
Assertions:	AM-03 The tool executes in execution environment XE. AO-12 If requested, a clone is created from an image file. AO-13 A clone is created using access interface DST-AI to write to the clone device. AO-14 If an unaligned clone is created, each sector written to the clone is accurately written to the same disk address on the clone that the sector occupied on the digital source. AO-17 If requested, any excess sectors on a clone destination device are not modified. AO-23 If the tool logs any log significant information, the information is accurately recorded in the log file.
Tester Name:	csr
Test Host:	DeathStar
Test Date:	Thu Mar 15 13:27:43 2012
Drives:	src(01-SATA) dst (50-SATA) other (none)
Source Setup:	src hash (SHA256): < 1AA01FEAE55F5CD55185D2B1A1359B3F913E7093FEF1D1ADA220CAC456BA40D8 > src hash (SHA1): < 4951236428C36B944E62E8D65862DCBEF05F282C > src hash (MD5): < 0A49B13D91FA9DA87CEEE9D006CB6FD6 > 156301488 total sectors (80026361856 bytes) Model (0JD-32HKA0) serial # (WD-WMAJ91448529)
Log Highlights:	====== Destination drive setup ====== 156301488 sectors wiped with 50 ====== Comparison of original to clone drive ====== Sectors compared: 156301488 Sectors match: 156301488 Sectors differ: 0 Bytes differ: 0 Diffs range 0 source read errors, 0 destination read errors
Results:	

Assertion & Expected Result	Actual Result
AM-03 Execution environment is XE.	as expected
AO-12 A clone is created from an image file.	as expected
AO-13 Clone created using interface AI.	as expected
AO-14 An unaligned clone is created.	as expected
AO-17 Excess sectors are unchanged.	as expected
AO-23 Logged information is correct.	as expected

Analysis:	Expected results achieved

5.2.44　　DA-14-NT

Test Case DA-14-NT AccessData FTK Imager CLI v2.9	
Case Summary:	DA-14 Create an unaligned clone from an image file.
Assertions:	AM-03 The tool executes in execution environment XE. AO-12 If requested, a clone is created from an image file. AO-13 A clone is created using access interface DST-AI to write to the clone device. AO-14 If an unaligned clone is created, each sector written to the clone is accurately written to the same disk address on the clone that the sector occupied on the digital source. AO-17 If requested, any excess sectors on a clone destination device are not modified. AO-23 If the tool logs any log significant information, the information is accurately recorded in the log file.
Tester Name:	csr
Test Host:	DeathStar
Test Date:	Thu Mar 22 15:25:08 2012
Drives:	src(01-IDE) dst (08-IDE) other (none)

Source Setup:	src hash (SHA1): < A48BB5665D6DC57C22DB68E2F723DA9AA8DF82B9 >
	src hash (MD5): < F458F673894753FA6A0EC8B8EC63848E >
	78165360 total sectors (40020664320 bytes)
	Model (0BB-00JHC0) serial # (WD-WMAMC74171)
	<pre>N Start LBA Length Start C/H/S End C/H/S boot Partition type
	 1 P 000000063 020980827 0000/001/01 1023/254/63 0C Fat32X
	 2 X 020980890 057175335 1023/000/01 1023/254/63 0F extended
	 3 S 000000063 000032067 1023/001/01 1023/254/63 01 Fat12
	 4 x 000032130 002104515 1023/000/01 1023/254/63 05 extended
	 5 S 000000063 002104452 1023/001/01 1023/254/63 06 Fat16
	 6 x 002136645 004192965 1023/000/01 1023/254/63 05 extended
	 7 S 000000063 004192902 1023/001/01 1023/254/63 16 other
	 8 x 006329610 008401995 1023/000/01 1023/254/63 05 extended
	 9 S 000000063 008401932 1023/001/01 1023/254/63 0B Fat32
	10 x 014731605 010490445 1023/000/01 1023/254/63 05 extended
	11 S 000000063 010490382 1023/001/01 1023/254/63 83 Linux
	12 x 025222050 004209030 1023/000/01 1023/254/63 05 extended
	13 S 000000063 004208967 1023/001/01 1023/254/63 82 Linux swap
	14 x 029431080 027744255 1023/000/01 1023/254/63 05 extended
	15 S 000000063 027744192 1023/001/01 1023/254/63 07 NTFS
	16 S 000000000 000000000 0000/000/00 0000/000/00 00 empty entry
	17 P 000000000 000000000 0000/000/00 0000/000/00 00 empty entry
	18 P 000000000 000000000 0000/000/00 0000/000/00 00 empty entry
	 1 020980827 sectors 10742183424 bytes
	 3 000032067 sectors 16418304 bytes
	 5 002104452 sectors 1077479424 bytes
	 7 004192902 sectors 2146765824 bytes
	 9 008401932 sectors 4301789184 bytes
	11 010490382 sectors 5371075584 bytes
	13 004208967 sectors 2154991104 bytes
	15 027744192 sectors 14205026304 bytes
	01NT-md5 14205026303 92B27B30BEE8B0FFBA8C660FA1590D49</pre>

Log Highlights:	<pre>====== Destination drive setup ======
	78165360 sectors wiped with 8
	
	====== Comparison of original to clone drive ======
	Sectors compared: 27744192
	Sectors match: 27744192
	Sectors differ: 0
	Bytes differ: 0
	Diffs range:
	run start Fri Mar 23 14:47:52 2012
	run finish Fri Mar 23 15:00:25 2012
	elapsed time 0:12:33
	Normal exit</pre>

Test Case DA-14-NT AccessData FTK Imager CLI v2.9	
	====== Tool Settings: ====== fill: none OS: Linux debian 2.6.32-5-486 #1 Mon Oct 3 03:34:28 UTC 2011 i686 GNU/Linux
Results:	

Assertion & Expected Result	Actual Result
AM-03 Execution environment is XE.	as expected
AO-12 A clone is created from an image file.	as expected
AO-13 Clone created using interface AI.	as expected
AO-14 An unaligned clone is created.	as expected
AO-17 Excess sectors are unchanged.	as expected
AO-23 Logged information is correct.	as expected

Analysis:	Expected results achieved

5.2.45   DA-14-S01

Test Case DA-14-S01 AccessData FTK Imager CLI v2.9	
Case Summary:	DA-14 Create an unaligned clone from an image file.
Assertions:	AM-03 The tool executes in execution environment XE. AO-12 If requested, a clone is created from an image file. AO-13 A clone is created using access interface DST-AI to write to the clone device. AO-14 If an unaligned clone is created, each sector written to the clone is accurately written to the same disk address on the clone that the sector occupied on the digital source. AO-17 If requested, any excess sectors on a clone destination device are not modified. AO-23 If the tool logs any log significant information, the information is accurately recorded in the log file.
Tester Name:	csr
Test Host:	DeathStar
Test Date:	Wed Apr 5 13:48:38 2012
Drives:	src(41) dst (6f) other (none)
Source Setup:	src hash (SHA256): < FBF3AA21489653D880FFAE71449A9F7E8EE4F56A6C3BF58A3A3FFB13203F1B1D > src hash (SHA1): < 15CAA1A307271160D8372668BF8A03FC45A51CC9 > src hash (MD5): < 0A6A8EF78BDC14E2026710D8CCB5607C > 78125000 total sectors (40000000000 bytes) 65534/015/63 (max cyl/hd values) 65535/016/63 (number of cyl/hd) IDE disk: Model (WDC WD400BB-75JHC0) serial # (WD-WMAMC4658355) N Start LBA Length Start C/H/S End C/H/S boot Partition type 1 P 000000063 078107967 0000/001/01 1023/254/63 Boot 07 NTFS 2 P 000000000 000000000 0000/000/00 0000/000/00 00 empty entry 3 P 000000000 000000000 0000/000/00 0000/000/00 00 empty entry 4 P 000000000 000000000 0000/000/00 0000/000/00 00 empty entry 1 078107967 sectors 39991279104 bytes
Log Highlights:	====== Destination drive setup ====== 120103200 sectors wiped with 6F ====== Comparison of original to clone drive ====== Sectors compared: 78125000 Sectors match: 78125000 Sectors differ: 0 Bytes differ: 0 Diffs range Source (78125000) has 41978200 fewer sectors than destination (120103200) Zero fill: 0 Src Byte fill (41): 0 Dst Byte fill (6F): 41978200 Other fill: 0 Other no fill: 0 Zero fill range: Src fill range: Dst fill range: 78125000-120103199 Other fill range: Other not filled range: 0 source read errors, 0 destination read errors ====== Tool Settings: ====== fill: none OS: Linux
Results:	

Assertion & Expected Result	Actual Result
AM-03 Execution environment is XE.	as expected

Test Case DA-14-S01 AccessData FTK Imager CLI v2.9		
	AO-12 A clone is created from an image file.	as expected
	AO-13 Clone created using interface AI.	as expected
	AO-14 An unaligned clone is created.	as expected
	AO-17 Excess sectors are unchanged.	as expected
	AO-23 Logged information is correct.	as expected
Analysis:	Expected results achieved	

5.2.46   DA-14-SATA28

Test Case DA-14-SATA28 AccessData FTK Imager CLI v2.9	
Case Summary:	DA-14 Create an unaligned clone from an image file.
Assertions:	AM-03 The tool executes in execution environment XE. AO-12 If requested, a clone is created from an image file. AO-13 A clone is created using access interface DST-AI to write to the clone device. AO-14 If an unaligned clone is created, each sector written to the clone is accurately written to the same disk address on the clone that the sector occupied on the digital source. AO-17 If requested, any excess sectors on a clone destination device are not modified. AO-23 If the tool logs any log significant information, the information is accurately recorded in the log file.
Tester Name:	csr
Test Host:	DeathStar
Test Date:	Thu Mar 8 15:10:51 2012
Drives:	src(4B-SATA) dst (22-IDE) other (none)
Source Setup:	src hash (SHA256): < F61ADE21982F803F64D2CEA2C9CA90C23056CA852CCC515D17827038154E8C1E > src hash (SHA1): < 70CC62B43F6A41CA4D6760AA0B9B4C415D3F48E2 > src hash (MD5): < 746B4C06CDD5FBD67C0820DB4325B40C > 156301488 total sectors (80026361856 bytes) Model (ST380815AS) serial # (6QZ5C9V5) N Start LBA Length Start C/H/S End C/H/S boot Partition type 1 P 000000063 020971520 0000/001/01 1023/254/63 AF other 2 P 020971629 010485536 1023/254/63 1023/254/63 AF other 3 P 031457223 006291456 1023/254/63 1023/254/63 A8 other 4 X 037748679 008388694 1023/254/63 1023/254/63 05 extended 5 S 000000039 004194304 1023/254/63 1023/254/63 AF other 6 x 004194343 004194351 1023/254/63 1023/254/63 05 extended 7 S 000000047 004194304 1023/254/63 1023/254/63 AF other 8 S 000000000 000000000 0000/000/00 0000/000/00 00 empty entry 1 020971520 sectors 10737418240 bytes 2 010485536 sectors 5368594432 bytes 3 006291456 sectors 3221225472 bytes 5 004194304 sectors 2147483648 bytes 7 004194304 sectors 2147483648 bytes
Log Highlights:	====== Destination drive setup ====== 195813072 sectors wiped with 22 ====== Comparison of original to clone drive ====== Sectors compared: 156301488 Sectors match: 156301488 Sectors differ: 0 Bytes differ: 0 Diffs range Source (156301488) has 39511584 fewer sectors than destination (195813072) Zero fill: 0 Src Byte fill (4B): 0 Dst Byte fill (22): 39511584 Other fill: 0 Other no fill: 0 Zero fill range: Src fill range: Dst fill range: 156301488-195813071 Other fill range: Other not filled range: 0 source read errors, 0 destination read errors ====== Tool Settings: ====== fill: none

Test Case DA-14-SATA28 AccessData FTK Imager CLI v2.9	
	OS: Linux ubuntu 2.6.32-33-generic #70-Ubuntu SMP Thu Jul 7 21:09:46 UTC 2011 i686 GNU/Linux
Results:	

Assertion & Expected Result	Actual Result
AM-03 Execution environment is XE.	as expected
AO-12 A clone is created from an image file.	as expected
AO-13 Clone created using interface AI.	as expected
AO-14 An unaligned clone is created.	as expected
AO-17 Excess sectors are unchanged.	as expected
AO-23 Logged information is correct.	as expected

Analysis:	Expected results achieved

5.2.47　　DA-14-SATA48

Test Case DA-14-SATA48 AccessData FTK Imager CLI v2.9	
Case Summary:	DA-14 Create an unaligned clone from an image file.
Assertions:	AM-03 The tool executes in execution environment XE. AO-12 If requested, a clone is created from an image file. AO-13 A clone is created using access interface DST-AI to write to the clone device. AO-14 If an unaligned clone is created, each sector written to the clone is accurately written to the same disk address on the clone that the sector occupied on the digital source. AO-17 If requested, any excess sectors on a clone destination device are not modified. AO-23 If the tool logs any log significant information, the information is accurately recorded in the log file.
Tester Name:	csr
Test Host:	DeathStar
Test Date:	Mon Mar 12 06:32:40 2012
Drives:	src(16-SATA) dst (22-LAP) other (none)
Source Setup:	src hash (SHA1): < F82982A9C63133988C1D2B4DA7C9C25CCA2D77A5 > src hash (MD5): < 7BB1D64D47671ED3E69130A2AD08FA02 > 312581808 total sectors (160041885696 bytes) 19456/254/63 (max cyl/hd values) 19457/255/63 (number of cyl/hd) Model (WDC WD1600JD-00G) serial # (WD-WMAES2058252) 　N　　Start LBA Length　　　Start C/H/S End C/H/S　　boot Partition type 　1 P 000000063 312560577 0000/001/01 1023/254/63 Boot 07 NTFS 　2 P 000000000 000000000 0000/000/00 0000/000/00　　00 empty entry 　3 P 000000000 000000000 0000/000/00 0000/000/00　　00 empty entry 　4 P 000000000 000000000 0000/000/00 0000/000/00　　00 empty entry 　1 312560577 sectors 160031015424 bytes
Log Highlights:	====== Destination drive setup ====== 312581808 sectors wiped with 22 ====== Comparison of original to clone drive ====== Sectors compared: 312581808 Sectors match:　　312581808 Sectors differ:　　　　0 Bytes differ:　　　　　0 Diffs range 0 source read errors, 0 destination read errors OS: Linux ubuntu 2.6.32-33-generic #70-Ubuntu SMP Thu Jul 7 21:09:46 UTC 2011 i686 GNU/Linux
Results:	<table><tr><th>Assertion & Expected Result</th><th>Actual Result</th></tr><tr><td>AM-03 Execution environment is XE.</td><td>as expected</td></tr><tr><td>AO-12 A clone is created from an image file.</td><td>as expected</td></tr><tr><td>AO-13 Clone created using interface AI.</td><td>as expected</td></tr><tr><td>AO-14 An unaligned clone is created.</td><td>as expected</td></tr><tr><td>AO-17 Excess sectors are unchanged.</td><td>as expected</td></tr><tr><td>AO-23 Logged information is correct.</td><td>as expected</td></tr></table>
Analysis:	Expected results achieved

5.2.48　DA-14-SCSI

Test Case DA-14-SCSI AccessData FTK Imager CLI v2.9	
Case Summary:	DA-14 Create an unaligned clone from an image file.
Assertions:	AM-03 The tool executes in execution environment XE. AO-12 If requested, a clone is created from an image file. AO-13 A clone is created using access interface DST-AI to write to the clone device. AO-14 If an unaligned clone is created, each sector written to the clone is accurately written to the same disk address on the clone that the sector occupied on the digital source. AO-17 If requested, any excess sectors on a clone destination device are not modified. AO-23 If the tool logs any log significant information, the information is accurately recorded in the log file.
Tester Name:	csr
Test Host:	Frank
Test Date:	Wed Apr 18 15:54:12 2012
Drives:	src(E0) dst (8F) other ()
Source Setup:	src hash (SHA1): < 4A6941F1337A8A22B10FC844B4D7FA6158BECB82 > src hash (MD5): < A97C8F36B7AC9D5233B90AC09284F938 > 17938985 total sectors (9184760320 bytes) Model (ATLAS10K2-TY092J) serial # (169028142436)
Log Highlights:	====== Destination drive setup ====== 39102336 sectors wiped with 8F ====== Comparison of original to clone drive ====== Sectors compared: 17938985 Sectors match: 17938985 Sectors differ: 0 Bytes differ: 0 Diffs range Source (17938985) has 21163351 fewer sectors than destination (39102336) Zero fill: 0 Src Byte fill (E0): 0 Dst Byte fill (8F): 21163351 Other fill: 0 Other no fill: 0 Zero fill range: Src fill range: Dst fill range: 17938985-39102335 Other fill range: Other not filled range: 0 source read errors, 0 destination read errors ====== Tool Settings: ====== fill: none OS: Linux ubuntu 2.6.32-33-generic #70-Ubuntu SMP Thu Jul 7 21:09:46 UTC 2011 i686 GNU/Linux
Results:	

Assertion & Expected Result	Actual Result
AM-03 Execution environment is XE.	as expected
AO-12 A clone is created from an image file.	as expected
AO-13 Clone created using interface AI.	as expected
AO-14 An unaligned clone is created.	as expected
AO-17 Excess sectors are unchanged.	as expected
AO-23 Logged information is correct.	as expected

Analysis:	Expected results achieved

5.2.49 DA-14-THUMB

Test Case DA-14-THUMB AccessData FTK Imager CLI v2.9	
Case Summary:	DA-14 Create an unaligned clone from an image file.
Assertions:	AM-03 The tool executes in execution environment XE. AO-12 If requested, a clone is created from an image file. AO-13 A clone is created using access interface DST-AI to write to the clone device. AO-14 If an unaligned clone is created, each sector written to the clone is accurately written to the same disk address on the clone that the sector occupied on the digital source. AO-17 If requested, any excess sectors on a clone destination device are not modified. AO-23 If the tool logs any log significant information, the information is accurately recorded in the log file.
Tester Name:	csr
Test Host:	DeathStar
Test Date:	Mon Mar 26 10:24:51 2012
Drives:	src(D5-Thumb) dst (D4-Thumb) other (none)
Source Setup:	src hash (SHA1): < D68520EF74A336E49DCCF83815B7B08FDC53E38A > src hash (MD5): < C843593624B2B3B878596D8760B19954 > 505856 total sectors (258998272 bytes) Model (usb2.0Flash Disk) serial # ()
Log Highlights:	====== Destination drive setup ====== 505856 sectors wiped with D4 ====== Comparison of original to clone drive ====== Sectors compared: 505856 Sectors match: 505856 Sectors differ: 0 Bytes differ: 0 Diffs range 0 source read errors, 0 destination read errors OS: Linux debian 2.6.32-5-486 #1 Mon Oct 3 03:34:28 UTC 2011 i686 GNU/Linux
Results:	

Assertion & Expected Result	Actual Result
AM-03 Execution environment is XE.	as expected
AO-12 A clone is created from an image file.	as expected
AO-13 Clone created using interface AI.	as expected
AO-14 An unaligned clone is created.	as expected
AO-17 Excess sectors are unchanged.	as expected
AO-23 Logged information is correct.	as expected

Analysis:	Expected results achieved

5.2.50 DA-14-USB

Test Case DA-14-USB AccessData FTK Imager CLI v2.9	
Case Summary:	DA-14 Create an unaligned clone from an image file.
Assertions:	AM-03 The tool executes in execution environment XE. AO-12 If requested, a clone is created from an image file. AO-13 A clone is created using access interface DST-AI to write to the clone device. AO-14 If an unaligned clone is created, each sector written to the clone is accurately written to the same disk address on the clone that the sector occupied on the digital source. AO-17 If requested, any excess sectors on a clone destination device are not modified. AO-23 If the tool logs any log significant information, the information is accurately recorded in the log file.
Tester Name:	csr
Test Host:	DeathStar
Test Date:	Wed Jul 25 16:11:45 2012
Drives:	src(63-FU2) dst (6F) other (none)
Source Setup:	src hash (SHA256): < EC8EF011494BA6DA18F74C47547C3E74E7180585096A830F9247A98EF613BB1D > src hash (SHA1): < F7069EDCBEAC863C88DECED82159F22DA96BE99B > src hash (MD5): < EE217BC4FA4F3D1B4021D29B065AA9EC > 117304992 total sectors (60060155904 bytes) Model (SP0612N) serial # () N Start LBA Length Start C/H/S End C/H/S boot Partition type 1 P 000000063 004192902 0000/001/01 0260/254/63 Boot 06 Fat16 2 X 004192965 113097600 0261/000/01 1023/254/63 0F extended 3 S 000000063 113097537 0261/001/01 1023/254/63 0B Fat32 4 S 000000000 000000000 0000/000/00 0000/000/00 00 empty entry 5 P 000000000 000000000 0000/000/00 0000/000/00 00 empty entry 6 P 000000000 000000000 0000/000/00 0000/000/00 00 empty entry 1 004192902 sectors 2146765824 bytes 3 113097537 sectors 57905938944 bytes
Log Highlights:	====== Destination drive setup ====== 120103200 sectors wiped with 6F ====== Comparison of original to clone drive ====== Sectors compared: 117304992 Sectors match: 117304992 Sectors differ: 0 Bytes differ: 0 Diffs range Source (117304992) has 2798208 fewer sectors than destination (120103200) Zero fill: 0 Src Byte fill (62): 0 Dst Byte fill (6F): 2798208 Other fill: 0 Other no fill: 0 Zero fill range: Src fill range: Dst fill range: 117304992-120103199 Other fill range: Other not filled range: 0 source read errors, 0 destination read errors
Results:	

Assertion & Expected Result	Actual Result
AM-03 Execution environment is XE.	as expected
AO-12 A clone is created from an image file.	as expected
AO-13 Clone created using interface AI.	as expected
AO-14 An unaligned clone is created.	as expected
AO-17 Excess sectors are unchanged.	as expected
AO-23 Logged information is correct.	as expected

Test Case DA-14-USB AccessData FTK Imager CLI v2.9	
Analysis:	Expected results achieved

5.2.51   DA-17

Test Case DA-17 AccessData FTK Imager CLI v2.9	
Case Summary:	DA-17 Create a truncated clone from an image file.
Assertions:	AM-03 The tool executes in execution environment XE. AO-12 If requested, a clone is created from an image file. AO-13 A clone is created using access interface DST-AI to write to the clone device. AO-19 If there is insufficient space to create a complete clone, a truncated clone is created using all available sectors of the clone device. AO-20 If a truncated clone is created, the tool notifies the user. AO-23 If the tool logs any log significant information, the information is accurately recorded in the log file.
Tester Name:	csr
Test Host:	DeathStar
Test Date:	Wed Mar 21 11:20:00 2012
Drives:	src(41) dst (31-IDE) other (none)
Source Setup:	src hash (SHA256): < FBF3AA21489653D880FFAE71449A9F7E8EE4F56A6C3BF58A3A3FFB13203F1B1D > src hash (SHA1): < 15CAA1A307271160D8372668BF8A03FC45A51CC9 > src hash (MD5): < 0A6A8EF78BDC14E2026710D8CCB5607C > 78125000 total sectors (40000000000 bytes) 65534/015/63 (max cyl/hd values) 65535/016/63 (number of cyl/hd) IDE disk: Model (WDC WD400BB-75JHC0) serial # (WD-WMAMC4658355) N Start LBA Length Start C/H/S End C/H/S boot Partition type 1 P 000000063 078107967 0000/001/01 1023/254/63 Boot 07 NTFS 2 P 000000000 000000000 0000/000/00 0000/000/00 00 empty entry 3 P 000000000 000000000 0000/000/00 0000/000/00 00 empty entry 4 P 000000000 000000000 0000/000/00 0000/000/00 00 empty entry 1 078107967 sectors 39991279104 bytes
Log Highlights:	====== Destination drive setup ====== 35673120 sectors wiped with 31 ====== Comparison of original to clone drive ====== Sectors compared: 35673120 Sectors match: 35673120 Sectors differ: 0 Bytes differ: 0 Diffs range Source (78125000) has 42451880 more sectors than destination (35673120) 0 source read errors, 0 destination read errors ====== Tool Message: ====== no message Write Block: 3 FASTBloc IDE OS: Linux debian 2.6.32-5-486 #1 Mon Oct 3 03:34:28 UTC 2011 i686 GNU/Linux
Results:	<table><tr><th>Assertion & Expected Result</th><th>Actual Result</th></tr><tr><td>AM-03 Execution environment is XE.</td><td>as expected</td></tr><tr><td>AO-12 A clone is created from an image file.</td><td>as expected</td></tr><tr><td>AO-13 Clone created using interface AI.</td><td>as expected</td></tr><tr><td>AO-19 Truncated clone is created.</td><td>as expected</td></tr><tr><td>AO-20 User notified that clone is truncated.</td><td>No Message</td></tr><tr><td>AO-23 Logged information is correct.</td><td>as expected</td></tr></table>
Analysis:	Expected results not achieved

5.2.52 DA-24

Test Case DA-24 AccessData FTK Imager CLI v2.9	
Case Summary:	DA-24 Verify a valid image.
Assertions:	AM-03 The tool executes in execution environment XE. AO-06 If the tool performs an image file integrity check on an image file that has not been changed since the file was created, the tool shall notify the user that the image file has not been changed. AO-23 If the tool logs any log significant information, the information is accurately recorded in the log file.
Tester Name:	csr
Test Host:	DeathStar
Test Date:	Wed Mar 21 07:17:53 2012
Drives:	src(41) dst (none) other (05-SATA)
Source Setup:	src hash (SHA256): < FBF3AA21489653D880FFAE71449A9F7E8EE4F56A6C3BF58A3A3FFB13203F1B1D > src hash (SHA1): < 15CAA1A307271160D8372668BF8A03FC45A51CC9 > src hash (MD5): < 0A6A8EF78BDC14E2026710D8CCB5607C > 78125000 total sectors (40000000000 bytes) 65534/015/63 (max cyl/hd values) 65535/016/63 (number of cyl/hd) IDE disk: Model (WDC WD400BB-75JHC0) serial # (WD-WMAMC4658355) N Start LBA Length Start C/H/S End C/H/S boot Partition type 1 P 000000063 078107967 0000/001/01 1023/254/63 Boot 07 NTFS 2 P 000000000 000000000 0000/000/00 0000/000/00 00 empty entry 3 P 000000000 000000000 0000/000/00 0000/000/00 00 empty entry 4 P 000000000 000000000 0000/000/00 0000/000/00 00 empty entry 1 078107967 sectors 39991279104 bytes

Log Highlights:	`------ Tool Message: ======`
	`root@debian:/media/xxx# ftkimager da-24.s01 --verify`
	`AccessData FTK Imager v2.9 CLI (May 12 2010)`
	`Copyright 2006-2010 AccessData Corp., 384 South 400 West, Lindon, UT 84042`
	`All rights reserved.`
	
	`Verifying image...`
	`Image verification complete.`
	`[MD5]`
	`  Computed hash: 0a6a8ef78bdc14e2026710d8ccb5607c`
	`  Image hash:    0a6a8ef78bdc14e2026710d8ccb5607c`
	`  Report hash:   0a6a8ef78bdc14e2026710d8ccb5607c`
	`  Verify result: Match`
	`[SHA1]`
	`  Computed hash: 15caa1a307271160d8372668bf8a03fc45a51cc9`
	`  Image hash:    15caa1a307271160d8372668bf8a03fc45a51cc9`
	`  Report hash:   15caa1a307271160d8372668bf8a03fc45a51cc9`
	`  Verify result: Match`
	
	`====== Tool Settings: ======`
	`image size: 947798213 MB`
	`image format: s01`
	
	`Write Block: 3 FASTBloc IDE`
	
	`OS: Linux debian 2.6.32-5-486 #1 Mon Oct 3 03:34:28 UTC 2011 i686 GNU/Linux`
	
	`====== Image file segments ======`
	`    1  947798213 Mar 21 09:57 da-24.s01`
	`    2       1098 Mar 21 10:00 da-24.s01.txt`
	`    3      16384 Mar 21  2012 lost+found`
	`    4          0 Mar 21 10:51 ls.txt`

Results:	

Assertion & Expected Result	Actual Result
AM-03 Execution environment is XE.	as expected

Test Case DA-24 AccessData FTK Imager CLI v2.9			
	AO-06 Tool verifies image file unchanged.	as expected	
	AO-23 Logged information is correct.	as expected	
Analysis:	Expected results achieved		

5.2.53 DA-25

Test Case DA-25 AccessData FTK Imager CLI v2.9	
Case Summary:	DA-25 Detect a corrupted image.
Assertions:	AM-03 The tool executes in execution environment XE. AO-07 If the tool performs an image file integrity check on an image file that has been changed since the file was created, the tool shall notify the user that the image file has been changed. AO-08 If the tool performs an image file integrity check on an image file that has been changed since the file was created, the tool shall notify the user of the affected locations. AO-23 If the tool logs any log significant information, the information is accurately recorded in the log file.
Tester Name:	csr
Test Host:	DeathStar
Test Date:	Mon Apr 2 09:03:43 2012
Drives:	src(D5-THUMB) dst (none) other (24-LAP)
Source Setup:	src hash (SHA1): < D68520EF74A336E49DCCF83815B7B08FDC53E38A > src hash (MD5): < C843593624B2B3B878596D8760B19954 > 505856 total sectors (258998272 bytes) Model (usb2.0Flash Disk) serial # ()

Log Highlights:	====== Image file corrupted for test run: ======
	Change byte 1028128 of file da-25.001 from 0x46 to 0x4E
	
	====== Tool Message: ======
	Verifying image...
	Image verification complete.
	[MD5]
	 Computed hash: e25e19f7b078cebbfbc6beffc1e29d38
	[SHA1]
	 Computed hash: 896a19d8d8318501ce3a3c36eee61c5c652420ba
	
	Write Block: 18 Tableau Forensic USB Bridge
	
	OS: Linux ubuntu 2.6.32-33-generic #70-Ubuntu SMP Thu Jul 7 21:09:46 UTC 2011 i686 GNU/Linux
	
	====== Image file segments ======
	    1 3854084 2012-04-02 09:10 da-25.E01
	    2 1094 2012-04-02 09:10 da-25.E01.txt
	    3 0 2012-04-02 09:10 ls.txt

Results:	

Assertion & Expected Result	Actual Result
AM-03 Execution environment is XE.	as expected
AO-07 User notified if image file has changed.	as expected
AO-08 User notified of changed locations.	as expected
AO-23 Logged information is correct.	as expected

Analysis:	Expected results achieved

5.2.54   DA-26-D2E

Test Case DA-26-D2E AccessData FTK Imager CLI v2.9	
Case Summary:	DA-26 Convert an image to an alternate image file format.
Assertions:	AM-03 The tool executes in execution environment XE. AO-09 If the tool converts a source image file from one format to a target image file in another format, the acquired data represented in the target image file is the same as the acquired data in the source image file. AO-23 If the tool logs any log significant information, the information is accurately recorded in the log file.
Tester Name:	csr
Test Host:	DeathStar
Test Date:	Tue Mar 27 14:06:48 2012
Drives:	src(D5-Thumb) dst (none) other (24-LAP)
Source Setup:	src hash (SHA1): < D68520EF74A336E49DCCF83815B7B08FDC53E38A > src hash (MD5): < C843593624B2B3B878596D8760B19954 > 505856 total sectors (258998272 bytes) Model (usb2.0Flash Disk) serial # ()

Log Highlights:	OS: Linux ubuntu 2.6.32-33-generic #70-Ubuntu SMP Thu Jul 7 21:09:46 UTC 2011 i686 GNU/Linux
	
	====== Image file segments ======
	    1 258998272 2012-04-03 12:55 da-26.001
	    2 258998784 2012-04-03 12:56 da-26E.001
	    3 976 2012-04-03 12:56 da-26E.001.txt
	    4 1094 2012-04-03 12:55 logfile.txt
	    5 0 2012-04-03 12:57 ls.txt
	======== Excerpt from Tool log ========
	Case: da-26-d2e
	Drive Geometry:
	 Cylinders: 1019
	 Heads: 8
	 Sectors per Track: 62
	 Bytes per Sector: 512
	 Sector Count: 505856
	Physical Drive Information:
	 Drive Model: CRUCIAL usb2.0Flash Disk
	 Drive Interface Type: SCSI
	 Source data size: 247 MB
	 Sector count: 505856
	Source hash:
	 MD5: c843593624b2b3b878596d8760b19954
	 SHA1: d68520ef74a336e49dccf83815b7b08fdc53e38a
	Verification hash:
	 MD5: c843593624b2b3b878596d8760b19954
	 SHA1: d68520ef74a336e49dccf83815b7b08fdc53e38a
	Segment list:
	 /media/xxx/da-26.001
	======== End of Excerpt from Tool log ========

Results:	

Assertion & Expected Result	Actual Result
AM-03 Execution environment is XE.	as expected
AO-09 Tool converts image file format.	as expected
AO-23 Logged information is correct.	as expected

Analysis:	Expected results achieved

5.2.55 DA-26-D2E01

Test Case DA-26-D2E01 AccessData FTK Imager CLI v2.9	
Case Summary:	DA-26 Convert an image to an alternate image file format.
Assertions:	AM-03 The tool executes in execution environment XE. AO-09 If the tool converts a source image file from one format to a target image file in another format, the acquired data represented in the target image file is the same as the acquired data in the source image file. AO-23 If the tool logs any log significant information, the information is accurately recorded in the log file.
Tester Name:	csr
Test Host:	DeathStar
Test Date:	Tue Mar 27 14:06:48 2012
Drives:	src(D5-Thumb) dst (none) other (24-LAP)
Source Setup:	src hash (SHA1): < D68520EF74A336E49DCCF83815B7B08FDC53E38A > src hash (MD5): < C843593624B2B3B878596D8760B19954 > 505856 total sectors (258998272 bytes) Model (usb2.0Flash Disk) serial # ()

Log Highlights:	OS: Linux ubuntu 2.6.32-33-generic #70-Ubuntu SMP Thu Jul 7 21:09:46 UTC 2011 i686 GNU/Linux
	
	====== Image file segments ======
	    1 258998272 2012-04-03 13:22 da-26.001
	    2 3854088 2012-04-03 13:23 da-26e01.E01
	    3 984 2012-04-03 13:23 da-26e01.E01.txt
	    4 1094 2012-04-03 13:22 logfile.txt
	======== Excerpt from Tool log ========
	Case: da-26-d2e01
	Drive Geometry:
	 Cylinders: 1019
	 Heads: 8
	 Sectors per Track: 62
	 Bytes per Sector: 512
	 Sector Count: 505856
	Physical Drive Information:
	 Drive Model: CRUCIAL usb2.0Flash Disk
	 Drive Interface Type: SCSI
	 Source data size: 247 MB
	 Sector count: 505856
	Source hash:
	 MD5: c843593624b2b3b878596d8760b19954
	 SHA1: d68520ef74a336e49dccf83815b7b08fdc53e38a
	Verification hash:
	 MD5: c843593624b2b3b878596d8760b19954
	 SHA1: d68520ef74a336e49dccf83815b7b08fdc53e38a
	Segment list:
	 /media/xxx/da-26.001
	======== End of Excerpt from Tool log ========

Results:	

Assertion & Expected Result	Actual Result
AM-03 Execution environment is XE.	as expected
AO-09 Tool converts image file format.	as expected
AO-23 Logged information is correct.	as expected

Analysis:	Expected results achieved

5.2.56   DA-26-D2S01

Test Case DA-26-D2S01 AccessData FTK Imager CLI v2.9	
Case Summary:	DA-26 Convert an image to an alternate image file format.
Assertions:	AM-03 The tool executes in execution environment XE. AO-09 If the tool converts a source image file from one format to a target image file in another format, the acquired data represented in the target image file is the same as the acquired data in the source image file. AO-23 If the tool logs any log significant information, the information is accurately recorded in the log file.
Tester Name:	csr
Test Host:	DeathStar
Test Date:	Tue Mar 27 14:06:48 2012
Drives:	src(D5-Thumb) dst (none) other (24-LAP)
Source Setup:	src hash (SHA1): < D68520EF74A336E49DCCF83815B7B08FDC53E38A > src hash (MD5): < C843593624B2B3B878596D8760B19954 > 505856 total sectors (258998272 bytes) Model (usb2.0Flash Disk) serial # ()

Log Highlights:	OS: Linux ubuntu 2.6.32-33-generic #70-Ubuntu SMP Thu Jul 7 21:09:46 UTC 2011 i686 GNU/Linux
	
	====== Image file segments ======
	    1 258998272 2012-04-03 13:09 da-26.001
	    2 3853919 2012-04-03 13:11 da-26s01.s01
	    3 984 2012-04-03 13:11 da-26s01.s01.txt
	    4 1094 2012-04-03 13:09 logfile.txt
	======== Excerpt from Tool log ========
	Case: da-26-d2s01
	Drive Geometry:
	 Cylinders: 1019
	 Heads: 8
	 Sectors per Track: 62
	 Bytes per Sector: 512
	 Sector Count: 505856
	Physical Drive Information:
	 Drive Model: CRUCIAL usb2.0Flash Disk
	 Drive Interface Type: SCSI
	 Source data size: 247 MB
	 Sector count: 505856
	Source hash:
	 MD5: c843593624b2b3b878596d8760b19954
	 SHA1: d68520ef74a336e49dccf83815b7b08fdc53e38a
	Verification hash:
	 MD5: c843593624b2b3b878596d8760b19954
	 SHA1: d68520ef74a336e49dccf83815b7b08fdc53e38a
	Segment list:
	 /media/xxx/da-26.001
	======== End of Excerpt from Tool log ========

Results:	

Assertion & Expected Result	Actual Result
AM-03 Execution environment is XE.	as expected
AO-09 Tool converts image file format.	as expected
AO-23 Logged information is correct.	as expected

Analysis:	Expected results achieved

5.2.57 DA-26-E012D

Test Case DA-26-E012D AccessData FTK Imager CLI v2.9	
Case Summary:	DA-26 Convert an image to an alternate image file format.
Assertions:	AM-03 The tool executes in execution environment XE. AO-09 If the tool converts a source image file from one format to a target image file in another format, the acquired data represented in the target image file is the same as the acquired data in the source image file. AO-23 If the tool logs any log significant information, the information is accurately recorded in the log file.
Tester Name:	csr
Test Host:	DeathStar
Test Date:	Tue Mar 27 14:06:48 2012
Drives:	src(D5-Thumb) dst (none) other (24-LAP)
Source Setup:	src hash (SHA1): < D68520EF74A336E49DCCF83815B7B08FDC53E38A > src hash (MD5): < C843593624B2B3B878596D8760B19954 > 505856 total sectors (258998272 bytes) Model (usb2.0Flash Disk) serial # ()

Log Highlights:	OS: Linux ubuntu 2.6.32-33-generic #70-Ubuntu SMP Thu Jul 7 21:09:46 UTC 2011 i686 GNU/Linux
	
	====== Image file segments ======
	    1 258998272 2012-04-03 14:24 da-26.001
	    2 1350 2012-04-03 14:24 da-26.001.txt
	    3 3854086 2012-04-03 14:24 da-26.E01
	    4 1094 2012-04-03 14:24 logfile.txt
	    5 0 2012-04-03 14:25 ls.txt
	======== Excerpt from Tool log ========
	Case: da-26-e012d
	Drive Geometry:
	 Cylinders: 1019
	 Heads: 8
	 Sectors per Track: 62
	 Bytes per Sector: 512
	 Sector Count: 505856
	Physical Drive Information:
	 Drive Model: CRUCIAL usb2.0Flash Disk
	 Drive Interface Type: SCSI
	 Source data size: 247 MB
	 Sector count: 505856
	Source hash:
	 MD5: c843593624b2b3b878596d8760b19954
	 SHA1: d68520ef74a336e49dccf83815b7b08fdc53e38a
	Verification hash:
	 MD5: c843593624b2b3b878596d8760b19954
	 SHA1: d68520ef74a336e49dccf83815b7b08fdc53e38a
	Segment list:
	 /media/xxx/da-26.E01
	======== End of Excerpt from Tool log ========

Results:	

Assertion & Expected Result	Actual Result
AM-03 Execution environment is XE.	as expected
AO-09 Tool converts image file format.	as expected
AO-23 Logged information is correct.	as expected

Analysis:	Expected results achieved

5.2.58　DA-26-E012E

Test Case DA-26-E012E AccessData FTK Imager CLI v2.9	
Case Summary:	DA-26 Convert an image to an alternate image file format.
Assertions:	AM-03 The tool executes in execution environment XE. AO-09 If the tool converts a source image file from one format to a target image file in another format, the acquired data represented in the target image file is the same as the acquired data in the source image file. AO-23 If the tool logs any log significant information, the information is accurately recorded in the log file.
Tester Name:	csr
Test Host:	DeathStar
Test Date:	Tue Mar 27 14:06:48 2012
Drives:	src(D5-Thumb) dst (none) other (24-LAP)
Source Setup:	src hash (SHA1): < D68520EF74A336E49DCCF83815B7B08FDC53E38A > src hash (MD5): < C843593624B2B3B878596D8760B19954 > 505856 total sectors (258998272 bytes) Model (usb2.0Flash Disk) serial # ()

Log Highlights:	OS: Linux ubuntu 2.6.32-33-generic #70-Ubuntu SMP Thu Jul 7 21:09:46 UTC 2011 i686 GNU/Linux
	
	====== Image file segments ======
	    1 258998784 2012-04-03 14:34 da-26E.001
	    2 1348 2012-04-03 14:34 da-26E.001.txt
	    3 3854084 2012-04-03 14:32 da-26.E01
	    4 1094 2012-04-03 14:32 da-26.E01.txt
	======== Excerpt from Tool log ========
	Case: da-26-e012e
	Drive Geometry:
	 Cylinders: 1019
	 Heads: 8
	 Sectors per Track: 62
	 Bytes per Sector: 512
	 Sector Count: 505856
	Physical Drive Information:
	 Drive Model: CRUCIAL usb2.0Flash Disk
	 Drive Interface Type: SCSI
	 Source data size: 247 MB
	 Sector count: 505856
	Source hash:
	 MD5: c843593624b2b3b878596d8760b19954
	 SHA1: d68520ef74a336e49dccf83815b7b08fdc53e38a
	Verification hash:
	 MD5: c843593624b2b3b878596d8760b19954
	 SHA1: d68520ef74a336e49dccf83815b7b08fdc53e38a
	Segment list:
	 /media/xxx/da-26.E01
	======== End of Excerpt from Tool log ========

Results:	

Assertion & Expected Result	Actual Result
AM-03 Execution environment is XE.	as expected
AO-09 Tool converts image file format.	as expected
AO-23 Logged information is correct.	as expected

Analysis:	Expected results achieved

5.2.59   DA-26-E012S01

Test Case DA-26-E012S01 AccessData FTK Imager CLI v2.9	
Case Summary:	DA-26 Convert an image to an alternate image file format.
Assertions:	AM-03 The tool executes in execution environment XE. AO-09 If the tool converts a source image file from one format to a target image file in another format, the acquired data represented in the target image file is the same as the acquired data in the source image file. AO-23 If the tool logs any log significant information, the information is accurately recorded in the log file.
Tester Name:	csr
Test Host:	DeathStar
Test Date:	Tue Mar 27 14:06:48 2012
Drives:	src(D5-Thumb) dst (none) other (24-LAP)
Source Setup:	src hash (SHA1): < D68520EF74A336E49DCCF83815B7B08FDC53E38A > src hash (MD5): < C843593624B2B3B878596D8760B19954 > 505856 total sectors (258998272 bytes) Model (usb2.0Flash Disk) serial # ()

Log Highlights:	OS: Linux ubuntu 2.6.32-33-generic #70-Ubuntu SMP Thu Jul 7 21:09:46 UTC 2011 i686 GNU/Linux
	
	====== Image file segments ======
	    1 3854090 2012-04-03 14:39 da-26.E01
	    2 3853919 2012-04-03 14:40 da-26.s01
	    3 1350 2012-04-03 14:40 da-26.s01.txt
	    4 1094 2012-04-03 14:39 logfile.txt
	======== Excerpt from Tool log ========
	Case: da-26-e012s01
	Drive Geometry:
	 Cylinders: 1019
	 Heads: 8
	 Sectors per Track: 62
	 Bytes per Sector: 512
	 Sector Count: 505856
	Physical Drive Information:
	 Drive Model: CRUCIAL usb2.0Flash Disk
	 Drive Interface Type: SCSI
	 Source data size: 247 MB
	 Sector count: 505856
	Source hash:
	 MD5: c843593624b2b3b878596d8760b19954
	 SHA1: d68520ef74a336e49dccf83815b7b08fdc53e38a
	Verification hash:
	 MD5: c843593624b2b3b878596d8760b19954
	 SHA1: d68520ef74a336e49dccf83815b7b08fdc53e38a
	Segment list:
	  /media/xxx/da-26.E01
	======== End of Excerpt from Tool log ========

Results:	

Assertion & Expected Result	Actual Result
AM-03 Execution environment is XE.	as expected
AO-09 Tool converts image file format.	as expected
AO-23 Logged information is correct.	as expected

Analysis:	Expected results achieved

5.2.60 DA-26-S012D

Test Case DA-26-S012D AccessData FTK Imager CLI v2.9	
Case Summary:	DA-26 Convert an image to an alternate image file format.
Assertions:	AM-03 The tool executes in execution environment XE. AO-09 If the tool converts a source image file from one format to a target image file in another format, the acquired data represented in the target image file is the same as the acquired data in the source image file. AO-23 If the tool logs any log significant information, the information is accurately recorded in the log file.
Tester Name:	csr
Test Host:	DeathStar
Test Date:	Tue Mar 27 14:06:48 2012
Drives:	src(D5-Thumb) dst (none) other (24-LAP)
Source Setup:	src hash (SHA1): < D68520EF74A336E49DCCF83815B7B08FDC53E38A > src hash (MD5): < C843593624B2B3B878596D8760B19954 > 505856 total sectors (258998272 bytes) Model (usb2.0Flash Disk) serial # ()

Log Highlights:	OS: Linux ubuntu 2.6.32-33-generic #70-Ubuntu SMP Thu Jul 7 21:09:46 UTC 2011 i686 GNU/Linux
	
	====== Image file segments ======
	    1 258998272 2012-04-03 14:50 da-26.001
	    2 1366 2012-04-03 14:50 da-26.001.txt
	    3 3853918 2012-04-03 14:49 da-26.s01
	    4 1094 2012-04-03 14:49 logfile.txt
	======== Excerpt from Tool log ========
	Case: da-26-s012d
	Drive Geometry:
	 Cylinders: 1019
	 Heads: 8
	 Sectors per Track: 62
	 Bytes per Sector: 512
	 Sector Count: 505856
	Physical Drive Information:
	 Drive Model: CRUCIAL usb2.0Flash Disk
	 Drive Interface Type: SCSI
	 Source data size: 247 MB
	 Sector count: 505856
	Source hash:
	 MD5: c843593624b2b3b878596d8760b19954
	 SHA1: d68520ef74a336e49dccf83815b7b08fdc53e38a
	Verification hash:
	 MD5: c843593624b2b3b878596d8760b19954
	 SHA1: d68520ef74a336e49dccf83815b7b08fdc53e38a
	Segment list:
	 /media/xxx/da-26.s01
	======== End of Excerpt from Tool log ========

Results:	

Assertion & Expected Result	Actual Result
AM-03 Execution environment is XE.	as expected
AO-09 Tool converts image file format.	as expected
AO-23 Logged information is correct.	as expected

Analysis:	Expected results achieved

5.2.61   DA-26-S012E

Test Case DA-26-S012E AccessData FTK Imager CLI v2.9	
Case Summary:	DA-26 Convert an image to an alternate image file format.
Assertions:	AM-03 The tool executes in execution environment XE. AO-09 If the tool converts a source image file from one format to a target image file in another format, the acquired data represented in the target image file is the same as the acquired data in the source image file. AO-23 If the tool logs any log significant information, the information is accurately recorded in the log file.
Tester Name:	csr
Test Host:	DeathStar
Test Date:	Tue Mar 27 14:06:48 2012
Drives:	src(D5-Thumb) dst (none) other (24-LAP)
Source Setup:	src hash (SHA1): < D68520EF74A336E49DCCF83815B7B08FDC53E38A > src hash (MD5): < C843593624B2B3B878596D8760B19954 > 505856 total sectors (258998272 bytes) Model (usb2.0Flash Disk) serial # ()

Log Highlights:	OS: Linux ubuntu 2.6.32-33-generic #70-Ubuntu SMP Thu Jul 7 21:09:46 UTC 2011 i686 GNU/Linux
	
	====== Image file segments ======
	    1 258998784 2012-04-03 14:45 da-26E.001
	    2 1364 2012-04-03 14:45 da-26E.001.txt
	    3 3853920 2012-04-03 14:44 da-26.s01
	    4 1094 2012-04-03 14:44 da-26.s01.txt
	======== Excerpt from Tool log ========
	Case: da-26-s012e
	Drive Geometry:
	 Cylinders: 1019
	 Heads: 8
	 Sectors per Track: 62
	 Bytes per Sector: 512
	 Sector Count: 505856
	Physical Drive Information:
	 Drive Model: CRUCIAL usb2.0Flash Disk
	 Drive Interface Type: SCSI
	 Source data size: 247 MB
	 Sector count: 505856
	Source hash:
	 MD5: c843593624b2b3b878596d8760b19954
	 SHA1: d68520ef74a336e49dccf83815b7b08fdc53e38a
	Verification hash:
	 MD5: c843593624b2b3b878596d8760b19954
	 SHA1: d68520ef74a336e49dccf83815b7b08fdc53e38a
	Segment list:
	 /media/xxx/da-26.s01
	======== End of Excerpt from Tool log ========

Results:	

Assertion & Expected Result	Actual Result
AM-03 Execution environment is XE.	as expected
AO-09 Tool converts image file format.	as expected
AO-23 Logged information is correct.	as expected

Analysis:	Expected results achieved

5.2.62   DA-26-S012E01

Test Case DA-26-S012E01 AccessData FTK Imager CLI v2.9	
Case Summary:	DA-26 Convert an image to an alternate image file format.
Assertions:	AM-03 The tool executes in execution environment XE. AO-09 If the tool converts a source image file from one format to a target image file in another format, the acquired data represented in the target image file is the same as the acquired data in the source image file. AO-23 If the tool logs any log significant information, the information is accurately recorded in the log file.
Tester Name:	csr
Test Host:	DeathStar
Test Date:	Tue Mar 27 14:06:48 2012
Drives:	src(D5-Thumb) dst (none) other (24-LAP)
Source Setup:	src hash (SHA1): < D68520EF74A336E49DCCF83815B7B08FDC53E38A > src hash (MD5): < C843593624B2B3B878596D8760B19954 > 505856 total sectors (258998272 bytes) Model (usb2.0Flash Disk) serial # ()

Log Highlights:	OS: Linux ubuntu 2.6.32-33-generic #70-Ubuntu SMP Thu Jul 7 21:09:46 UTC 2011 i686 GNU/Linux
	
	====== Image file segments ======
	    1 3854088 2012-04-03 14:54 da-26.E01
	    2 1366 2012-04-03 14:54 da-26.E01.txt
	    3 3853919 2012-04-03 14:54 da-26.s01
	    4 1094 2012-04-03 14:54 logfile.txt
	======== Excerpt from Tool log ========
	Case: da-26-s012e01
	Drive Geometry:
	 Cylinders: 1019
	 Heads: 8
	 Sectors per Track: 62
	 Bytes per Sector: 512
	 Sector Count: 505856
	Physical Drive Information:
	 Drive Model: CRUCIAL usb2.0Flash Disk
	 Drive Interface Type: SCSI
	 Source data size: 247 MB
	 Sector count: 505856
	Source hash:
	 MD5: c843593624b2b3b878596d8760b19954
	 SHA1: d68520ef74a336e49dccf83815b7b08fdc53e38a
	Verification hash:
	 MD5: c843593624b2b3b878596d8760b19954
	 SHA1: d68520ef74a336e49dccf83815b7b08fdc53e38a
	Segment list:
	 /media/xxx/da-26.s01
	======== End of Excerpt from Tool log ========

Results:	

Assertion & Expected Result	Actual Result
AM-03 Execution environment is XE.	as expected
AO-09 Tool converts image file format.	as expected
AO-23 Logged information is correct.	as expected

Analysis:	Expected results achieved

About the National Institute of Justice

A component of the Office of Justice Programs, NIJ is the research, development and evaluation agency of the U.S. Department of Justice. NIJ's mission is to advance scientific research, development and evaluation to enhance the administration of justice and public safety. NIJ's principal authorities are derived from the Omnibus Crime Control and Safe Streets Act of 1968, as amended (see 42 U.S.C. §§ 3721–3723).

The NIJ Director is appointed by the President and confirmed by the Senate. The Director establishes the Institute's objectives, guided by the priorities of the Office of Justice Programs, the U.S. Department of Justice, and the needs of the field. The Institute actively solicits the views of criminal justice and other professionals and researchers to inform its search for the knowledge and tools to guide policy and practice.

Strategic Goals

NIJ has seven strategic goals grouped into three categories:

Creating relevant knowledge and tools

1. Partner with state and local practitioners and policymakers to identify social science research and technology needs.
2. Create scientific, relevant, and reliable knowledge—with a particular emphasis on terrorism, violent crime, drugs and crime, cost-effectiveness, and community-based efforts—to enhance the administration of justice and public safety.
3. Develop affordable and effective tools and technologies to enhance the administration of justice and public safety.

Dissemination

4. Disseminate relevant knowledge and information to practitioners and policymakers in an understandable, timely and concise manner.
5. Act as an honest broker to identify the information, tools and technologies that respond to the needs of stakeholders.

Agency management

6. Practice fairness and openness in the research and development process.
7. Ensure professionalism, excellence, accountability, cost-effectiveness and integrity in the management and conduct of NIJ activities and programs.

Program Areas

In addressing these strategic challenges, the Institute is involved in the following program areas: crime control and prevention, including policing; drugs and crime; justice systems and offender behavior, including corrections; violence and victimization; communications and information technologies; critical incident response; investigative and forensic sciences, including DNA; less-than-lethal technologies; officer protection; education and training technologies; testing and standards; technology assistance to law enforcement and corrections agencies; field testing of promising programs; and international crime control.

In addition to sponsoring research and development and technology assistance, NIJ evaluates programs, policies, and technologies. NIJ communicates its research and evaluation findings through conferences and print and electronic media.

To find out more about the National Institute of Justice, please visit:

www.nij.gov

or contact:

National Criminal Justice
 Reference Service
P.O. Box 6000
Rockville, MD 20849–6000
800–851–3420
http://www.ncjrs.gov

www.ingramcontent.com/pod-product-compliance
Lightning Source LLC
Chambersburg PA
CBHW080259290526
45790CB00005B/1872